THE ADELAIDE HOSPITAL SCHOOL OF NURSING

This book is dedicated to all Adelaide nurses, past and present

Gerard M. Fealy

The Adelaide Hospital School of Nursing, 1859-2009

A COMMEMORATIVE HISTORY

the columba press

First published in 2009 by
the columba press
55A Spruce Avenue, Stillorgan Industrial Park, Blackrock, Co. Dublin

Cover by Bill Bolger
Origination by The Columba Press
Printed in Ireland by ColourBooks Ltd, Dublin

ISBN 978-1-85607-655-5

Table of Contents

Acknowledgements

I am indebted to the nurses who so generously gave oral and written testimony in the preparation of this book, and to the many past and present Adelaide nurses who generously offered documentary materials, photographs and other artefacts, many of which were used in researching and writing the book. I am also most grateful to the many individuals associated with the Adelaide Hospital who communicated support for the project.

I am indebted to Dr Bernard Meehan, Keeper of Manuscripts at Trinity College Dublin, and Estelle Gittins, archivist responsible for the Adelaide Hospital Archives for their guidance and support. I also extend my gratitude to all the staff at the Manuscripts Reading Room at Trinity, who offered their support and assistance during my many visits to the Adelaide archives. I am grateful to Hilary Daly for providing me with access to the Adelaide Nurses' League archives, and Catherine Talbot of the Meath Foundation for providing access to oral history materials recorded in 1998. I am grateful to Valerie Houlden and Yvonne Seville who gave copious documentary materials and photographs and to John Giles, Sunbeam House Services, for his generosity in providing valuable materials on Lucinda Sullivan. I am also grateful to Carol McCubbin and Kath Start of Kingston University for their advice and support, and to Ines Warsop for arranging transcription of the oral history interviews. I wish to acknowledge the expertise and assistance of the AMNCH Clinical Photography Department.

I am indebted to the Adelaide Hospital Society for their foresight in commissioning this book and, in so doing, for commemorating and celebrating the Adelaide nurse. In particular, I extend my gratitude to Society Chief Executive Róisín Whiting and former Chief Executive Dr Fergus O'Ferrall for their guidance and support. I am indebted to the members of the Adelaide Hospital School Commemorative Group, who supported me in researching and writing the book, collecting primary source materials, and offering suggestions and guidance throughout. The Group members were Dr Fergus O'Ferrall, Róisín Whiting, Shirley Ingram, Hilary Daly and Roslyn Garrett. Members of the Adelaide Nurses League, including Yvonne Seville, also provided important background support and advice throughout the project.

I am most grateful to Dr Fergus O'Ferrall and Shirley Ingram for their insightful comments and suggestions on the first draft of the manuscript.

I extend my gratitude to my all colleagues at the UCD School of Nursing, Midwifery & Health Systems for their support and encouragement for this project, including Dr Michelle Butler, Dean and Head of School, Professor Pearl Treacy, Dr Martin McNamara and Dr Therese Meehan, and Dr Judith Harford, UCD School of Education, and to Professor Cecily Begley and former colleagues at the School of Nursing & Midwifery, Trinity College Dublin.

I reserve my deepest gratitude for my wife Deirdre and my sons Mervyn and Jonathan for their unfailing love and support.

Preface

Established in 1859 as a training school for young Protestant women, the Adelaide Hospital School of Nursing in Dublin was the first nurse training school for lay women in Ireland. The school was an integral part of an institution founded to give 'medical attendance, and also pastoral support and consolation, exclusively to Protestants in reduced circumstances'. The Hospital's 'peculiar religious character' remained a fundamental part of its constitution, giving clear direction to its management policies and to its approaches to treatment and care.

For one hundred and fifty years, the Adelaide Hospital School of Nursing has trained nurses who provided 'assiduous and intelligent' nursing care to the people of Ireland. The Adelaide School developed a national reputation as a place for training nurses who excelled in their standards of nursing. The Adelaide Hospital's successful development as a modern teaching hospital was in great part attributable to the quality of the nursing care that was proffered by its nurses in their distinctive uniform of blue cotton with white hail spot.

In the nineteenth century, the Adelaide Hospital School was one of Dublin's most prominent training schools, and the hospital continued to lead the way in developing modern nursing methods and nurse training into the twentieth century. The hospital's nurses remained at the forefront of developments in nursing practice and professional training, both inside and outside the Adelaide up to the present day.

The 'dear old Adelaide' closed at Peter Street and became part of the new Adelaide and Meath Hospital, incorporating the National Children's Hospital at Tallaght in 1998. The Tallaght Hospital Charter provided the mechanism for the retention of the Adelaide's unique position as the focus for Protestant participation in the health services in Ireland, and it also enabled the continuation of the Adelaide School. Today, consistent with the provisions of the Charter, the Adelaide Hospital Society retains responsibility for selecting students for the new nursing degree programme at Trinity College Dublin, a responsibility that remains unique to the Adelaide Hospital Society.

Combining social, professional and institutional history, this book exam-ines the history of the Adelaide Hospital School, largely through a nursing lens. It is based on documentary primary sources contained in the archives of the Adelaide Hospital located at Trinity College Dublin and on oral and written testimonies generously given by former Adelaide nurses. In this way the experiences of nurses who trained and worked in the Adelaide feature in each chapter, and short biographies of significant players in the Adelaide nursing story are presented throughout.

Foreword

This history of the Adelaide Hospital School of Nursing is the first full scale scholarly study of one Irish nursing school. Irish nurses have achieved international respect for their caring, expertise, dedication and professionalism. Within this national tradition of Irish nursing the Adelaide School of Nursing has a fame 'peculiar' to itself. Much of what gave 'peculiar' characteristics to the Adelaide tradition of nursing arose from the Christian values embedded in the origin and development of the Adelaide Hospital. While such values were often expressed in the nineteenth century in an exclusive way they were deeply held and were lived out in nursing practice in a way in which our more secular culture (and perhaps more shallow age) can only with some difficulty appreciate. Gerard Fealy's book treats with skill and sensitivity the values which inspired early nurse leaders in the Adelaide and how later inclusivity and change was embraced by their successors. Christian values motivated, to take one example, Lucinda Sullivan not only in nursing care but also to pioneer badly needed social provision. This Christian and radical commitment to the poor and less well off is a significant part of the Adelaide tradition expressed also by some doctors such as Kathleen Lynn. This book helps us recover this part of the Adelaide heritage of caring and perhaps it is one which is most valuable to reflect on into the twenty-first century when there is so much concern for the loss of such values including love and care for others.

The development of the Adelaide School of Nursing since 1859 mirrors the changes in the Church of Ireland (and to a lesser extent the other Protestant Churches) in a period when Ireland moved from Union with Great Britain (and the Church of Ireland moved from being the Established Church to Disestablishment) in the Victorian hey-day to Independence, the establishment of the Republic and entry into the European Union. During this period of radical change in church and state the Adelaide School of Nursing was to the forefront in promoting the nursing profession whilst seeking to sustain the values it embodied. Gerard Fealy's book will become and remain the classic account of what was at times a heroic charitable endeavour – a voluntary contribution to healthcare which embraced support from parishes and individuals throughout Ireland. The first century of the Adelaide School of Nursing – to 1960 – was a century when the Adelaide Hospital was supported entirely by charitable funds.

This book will become the essential companion to the author's *A History of Apprenticeship Nursing in Ireland* (Routledge, London & New York, 2006), the definitive history of nurse education and development in Ireland. Both books are vital contributions to the development of published historical scholarship concerned with the history of Irish healthcare.

Today the Adelaide School of Nursing is a distinctive stream within the School of Nursing and Midwifery at Trinity College, Dublin and has a status within the Charter of the Adelaide & Meath Hospital, Dublin, incorporating the National Children's Hospital at Tallaght approved by the Oireachtas in 1996. The Adelaide Hospital Society exercises responsibility for admission to the Adelaide School of Nursing in conjunction with the Central Applications Office and Trinity College, Dublin. The Society continues to support student nurses with bursaries and scholarships and to award scholarships to nurses each year under the Board of the Adelaide School of Nursing, which reports to the Board of the Society. The distinctive 'hail spots' are worn by nursing students.

It is most important that nursing students of the twenty-first century learn about the caring contribution of their foremothers in the profession. With Gerard Fealy's comprehensive history of the Adelaide School, succeeding generations of nursing students will have easy access to the heritage of care in which they stand and which they may be able to develop even more richly in the future. We owe Professor Fealy an immense debt for undertaking this 'labour of love' and we appreciate the many Adelaide nurses and others who assisted him to produce such an attractive book. In the 1960s, as a schoolboy with a broken leg as a result of a rugby tackle, I first encountered the love and care of Adelaide nurses. In the name of all their patients down the years may I say a heartfelt 'thank-you' to all Adelaide nurses who provided not only 'assiduous and intelligent nursing' but loving personal care to so many for now over 150 years.

Dr Fergus O'Ferrall,
Adelaide Lecturer in Health Policy,
Department of Public Health & Primary Care,
Trinity College Dublin.

CHAPTER ONE

A Training Institution for Protestant Nurses

With its magnificent buildings, including the Parliament House, the Custom House, and the Royal Exchange, and its grand thoroughfare of Sackville Street, Dublin was one of the great cities of the Georgian era. However, with the Act of Union and the loss of the Irish Parliament in 1800, there followed a period of economic decline, with many of Dublin's wealthy families leaving for England or moving to new suburbs and abandoning their townhouse properties in the city centre.[1] Many of these same townhouses became tenement dwellings for the urban poor, and during the first half of the nineteenth century, the city centre had numerous poor districts with a high proportion of the population living in circumstances of abject poverty in overcrowded tenements, and experiencing poor sanitation, malnutrition, and susceptibility to infectious diseases.

The area around St Patrick's Cathedral, including Bride Street and Peter Street, was one of the poorest districts. Part of the 'old Liberties', the area was identified as one of the city's 'unhealthy areas' in the nineteenth century, with narrow streets and houses crowded together. The Rector of St Catherine's Church at Thomas Street, the Reverend James Whitelaw, described the conditions of the very poor of the Liberties:

Ten to sixteen persons of all ages and sexes [live] in a room not sixteen feet square, stretched without any covering, save the wretched rags that constituted their wearing apparel. This crowded population wherever it obtains is almost universally accompanied by a very serious evil – a degree of filth and stench inconceivable.[2]

This account gives evidence of the growing problem of tenement dwellings that were a constant part of life for the poor of Dublin. In these circumstances of overcrowding and lack of any proper systems of sanitation and waste disposal, epidemic diseases including typhus, cholera, measles and tuberculosis were ever present. Those poor who survived childhood illness, like measles and diphtheria, in adulthood were likely to experience 'fevers, diseases of the chest, acute and chronic, of the stomach and bowels, [and] rheumatic and dropsical complaints.'[3] Dublin's voluntary hospitals and its workhouse infirmaries catered for the city's sick poor, and even in the late nineteenth century, conditions for the very poor in the Liberties had not improved; among the area's notorious 'fever nests' identified by the city's Medical Officer of Health in 1876 were streets in the vicinity of St Patrick's Cathedral, including Patrick's Close, Liberty Lane, Wood Street, and Plunket Street.[4]

This situation of extreme urban poverty and related poor public health provided the impetus for the founding of the voluntary or 'charity' hospitals in the late eighteenth and early nineteenth centuries, as well as the establishment of special hospitals like the Cork Street Fever Hospital and the Westmorland Lock Hospital for the treatment of venereal diseases. The special hospitals, workhouse infirmaries, and the voluntary hospitals were the principal means of giving indoor medical relief to Dublin's urban poor at the time. Founded by Protestant philanthropists, the voluntary hospitals were also places where new advances in medical science were developed and tested and where modern nursing was established.[5]

The Adelaide Hospital

The idea of founding a hospital 'for the exclusive use of Protestants' was originated in the 1830s by Albert Jasper Walsh (1815–1880), the son of John Walsh Esq. of Dundrum Castle.[6] Still a medical student at the Royal College of Surgeons at the time when he first considered his plan, Albert was driven by strong religious conviction, and just two years after qualifying as a doctor, he founded 'the Adelaide Institution' in late 1838 with the support and assistance of his two brothers Frederick and John. Located in the south inner city at No 43 Bride Street, the 'Adelaide Institution and Protestant Hospital' received its first patients in early 1839, and from the outset was both a place of medical relief for the sick poor and a religious institution. In the words of its first elected physician, Dr James Foulis Duncan, the distinct role of the Hospital was '[to combine] in one Institution the two distinct objects of religious instruction and medical treatment.'[7]

The new Institution was named in honour of Queen Adelaide, Consort and later Queen Dowager to King William IV. Adelaide was the aunt of Queen Victoria, who succeeded William on his death in 1837, and as Queen Dowager, she was petitioned by the founders of the Adelaide Institution to act as its patroness. Queen Adelaide acceded to the request and she later donated a sum of £25 to the new institution, which would thereafter bear her name and whose coat of arms was derived from her coat of arms, and still remains the coat of arms of the Adelaide Hospital Society.[8] The name seemed most fitting for a charitable institution, since Queen Adelaide was a woman of great dignity and humility; on her death bed she declared that 'we are alike before the throne of God', and she willed that she should not have a state funeral but instead requested a funeral 'free from the vanities and pomp of this world.'[9]

Ten years at Bride Street

The early Victorian period was characterised by the proliferation of strict rules that were designed to govern people's lives and these rules were especially prominent in public institutions that housed the poor, such as charity hospitals and workhouses. The Ward Rules for the new Adelaide Institution typified the strict demands on the poor to act with propriety while in receipt of medical relief:

> Patients are required to behave with propriety and respect to all author-
> ised visitors and to give the strictest attention to the prayers and scrip-
> tures when read to them ... No communication whatever is permitted
> between the Male and Female Wards ... No patient [is] to go out with-
> out special permission from the medical attendant. Irregular habits,
> smoking, want of cleanliness, wilful injury to the clothes or furniture
> of the Hospital, with immoral or indelicate language, shall subject the
> offender to instant dismissal.[10]

Similar strict rules of behaviour applied to staff and servants of the hospital, including nurses and ward maids. A sense of the nature of nursing care, insofar as it existed at the time of the opening of the Adelaide, may be gleaned from the fact that convalescent patients were 'required to assist the nurses in all duties connected with the establishment, such as cleaning the wards, washing etc., at the desire of the Matron and the permission of the Medical Officer on duty.' The practice of requiring convalescent patients to assist the nurses in their work was common in the Dublin hospitals of the period, and it was from the ranks of convalescent patients that many of the hospital's nurses were drawn. The first Matron of the hospital was Mrs Harding, who held the position until 1848 when she resigned. Like her counterparts in the other charity hospitals, it may be assumed that Mrs Harding did not receive any formal training in the theory and practice of sick nursing, and her role was more that of manager of the hospital household, overseeing cooking, laundry, and ward supplies, and superintending female servants.

From the outset, the hospital endeavoured to 'give to the Poor Protestant (often a person fallen from the ranks of respectable society) an asylum in illness' and to furnish 'medical attendance, and also pastoral support and consolation, exclusively to Protestants in reduced circumstances', and it relied entirely on subscriptions and donations, including subscriptions from its attending medical officers. However, financial difficulties were an abiding concern for charity hospitals in Dublin in the period, and some few years after its founding, the new institution experienced the first of many financial crises in 1843 when its creditors, notably Captain Westlake, the landlord of the property at 43 Bride Street in which the hospital was located, demanded payment of rent overdue. The fact that the hospital had only twenty beds made it ineligible to receive paying medical pupils, and this greatly impacted on its ability to generate income. With valiant fundraising at this time, the hospital struggled on, but with deterioration in the condition of the building and ever worsening financial circumstances, the founders and managers of the hospital were forced to hand back the premises at Bride Street to the landlord in 1848.

Reopening at Peter Street

The effective closure of the Adelaide Hospital was a blow to its trustees and medical officers who had so desperately tried to secure new premises for the fledgling institution. However, the forced closure would not diminish the 'faith, courage and energy' to pursue the objectives of using monies donated by trustees to secure a building suitable for a hospital and of reopening and successfully managing the Adelaide Hospital.[11] The Adelaide remained closed for almost ten years before a suitable building was identified at nearby Peter Street in 1857. With monies given by a number of benefactors, including Lord Farnham, Miss Batt, the Misses Brooke and the Hon. Charles Crichton, as well as a Trust of over £1,000, the property of a Dr Verner at No 24 and that of a Mr Bewley at No 25 Peter Street were purchased in 1858. A nearby house at No 27 Peter Street was also taken by the physicians and surgeons for use as a hostel for medical pupils. In the following year, No 26 Peter Street was purchased. In use as stables, the property was later opened in 1861 as the Fever Shed. The future of the Adelaide Hospital was at that moment secure.

Fundamental principle

The motivations of the Adelaide Hospital's original founders in the mid-nineteenth century and their successors as guardians of the 'fundamental principle' upon which the hospital was founded gave rise to the hospital's 'peculiar features' as a public institution. The 'peculiar religious character' of the Adelaide was that it should remain 'an essentially Religious and

Protestant Institution', and a statement of this principle was carried in the annual reports of the hospital's Managing Committee:

> The fundamental principle upon which the Adelaide Hospital has been established being, that it should remain an essentially Religious and Protestant Institution, it is hereby declared, that in order to per-petuate its original constitution, no person shall at any time be eligi-ble to hold any appointment in connection therewith, or to vote or take part in any of its proceedings, or be permitted access to the Hospital to communicate religious instruction, or for any purpose of religion whatsoever, who is not a member of, or does not profess the doctrines of, the Protestant Reformed Churches.[12]

The fundamental principle remained an essential part of its constitution and gave direction to the hospital's Managing Committee, its officers and staff as to how it should be run, and it determined the rules that governed the admission of in-patients and the employment of officers and staff and servants of the hospital. In his history of the Adelaide, David Mitchell dis-cusses the reasons for the assertion of the fundamental principle, relating it to 'spiritual arousal and Protestant evangelical enthusiasm' in the face of a lax and lethargic Protestant hierarchy at that time. This evangelical enthusiasm included a hope of converting the Irish people to the reformed faith, but later in the nineteenth century, in the face of an increasingly confident Catholic Church, the position had become more one of concern to guard the Protestant religion in Ireland. Added to this was the fact that many Protestant poor resided in the nearby Liberties district of the city and were in great need of medical relief. Reflecting on the persistence of the fundamen-tal principle, Mitchell observes that it is unlikely that those drafting it had ever intended to refuse admittance to Roman Catholics, and it appears that the many public disputes that arose in relation to Catholic priests wishing to give religious instruction in the hospital resulted in a blanket refusal to admit Catholics.

Religious tensions were an abiding feature of public life in Dublin in this period; in evidence to the Select Committee on Dublin Hospitals in 1854, the prominent Dublin physician Dominic Corrigan admitted that 'religious dif-ferences have to do with everything in Ireland.'[13] Following Catholic eman-cipation, a mutual mistrust between Protestants and Catholics frequently found expression in accusations of proselytising by one side or the other. These accusations were frequently aired with reference to the giving of char-ity and medical relief, contexts in which it was feared the poor and the sick might be more susceptible to religious conversion. In the First Annual Report following the hospital's reopening at Peter Street, the Managing Committee of the Adelaide laid such an accusation at the door of one Dublin Catholic hospital:

> Experience has taught us that since 1839, the zeal of Rome to win pros-elytes has become more determined and unscrupulous than ever ... [and] every inducement will be furnished to draw in our Protestant poor, and place them under the agents of superstition.[14]

The hospital authorities declared their intention to maintain, 'with all credit, respectability, and efficiency, one Institution, which shall never be defiled by superstition and in which our Protestant brethren may enjoy spir-itual comfort and real liberty of conscience.' Being essentially religious and Protestant, the new Institution would afford 'bodily relief and spiritual com-fort' to Protestants, but it would 'never close its doors against others who may be desirous of its benefits, and who are willing to abide by its great principle.'[15]

At the official reopening of the Adelaide Hospital at Peter Street in 1858, James Foulis Duncan, physician to the hospital, gave the inaugural address to the gentlemen gathered in the hospital theatre.[16] One of the hospital's origi-nal medical officers from the Bride Street period, Dr Duncan opened his address by congratulating the friends and supporters of the hospital 'upon its altered circumstances in which it now emerges, from the chrysalis condition in which it has been long entombed.' He spoke of the new building that was now 'more respectable in appearance and more extensive in its accommod-ation [and] ... better adapted in every respect for the purpose for which it is intended.' While the old Hospital at Bride Street had secured 'the confidence of the sick poor who resorted to it for relief', the new hospital had 'provided for every convenience in the way of comfort and ventilation that the present state of medical science suggests as necessary or desirable.' The Adelaide was not only 'a temple dedicated to Science and Humanity, [but] ... an Institution consecrated to the still higher purposes of Religion and Faith.'

Medical relief and medical training

The year 1859 was significant in the annals of modern science. In that year Charles Darwin published *On the Origin of Species*, and with it one of the great discoveries of science. Darwin's theory was published only after many years of painstaking observation in the natural world. In that same year, Florence Nightingale had accumulated sufficient monies in the Nightingale Fund to establish her Nursing School at St Thomas's Hospital in London, which opened in 1860. Within a few short years, Pasteur's Germ Theory and Lister's principles of antisepsis would be published to an initially sceptical medical community. Nevertheless, the scientific method of discovery was firmly established as the basis for medicine and surgery at the time of the reopening of the Adelaide in 1858.

In its early years at Peter Street, the hospital was treating in excess of 1,000 inpatients a year from all parts of Ireland, and over 12,000 outpatients at the hospital's dispensary. The great majority of patients belonged to 'the very poor class' and were generally members of the families of 'small farmers, artisans, or servants'. For many, attendance at the Adelaide provided them with medical relief and prevented them from 'drifting into pauperism.'[17] In 1862, the hospital had capacity to treat one hundred inpatients. Medical cases treated at the time were predominantly fevers, including typhoid, scarlatina and measles, while surgical cases included injuries and ophthalmic and orthopaedic cases.

Along with their role in giving medical relief to the sick poor, the other important function of voluntary hospitals was the training of medical pupils, and later, the training of nurses. The voluntary hospitals and the medical schools were bound closely together, where it was recognised that '[medical] schools would not be complete without the hospitals; [and] the hospitals are an indispensable part of the [medical] school.'[18] The Adelaide Hospital was associated with the nearby private Ledwich School of Medicine, and later in 1889 when the Ledwich School closed, with the School of Physic at Trinity College Dublin.

In 1858, Dr Duncan lectured on the important part that clinical instruction played 'in the great scheme of medical education' and the importance of practical experience in the training of physicians, remarking that 'many of the symptoms of disease can only be learned at the bedside of the patient.'[19] He observed that changes in the way diseases were treated were the result of 'a conviction forced upon every unprejudiced physician by a careful observation of the facts before him.'[20] Later in 1864, Dr Duncan spoke of the importance of observation in the training of medical pupils, stating that the human senses were the 'essential, instruments for the detection of morbid phenomena.'[21] The Adelaide Hospital was at the forefront of many of the new developments in scientific medicine. Kendal Franks, the Adelaide surgeon, was one of the first medical men in Dublin to accept Pasteur's new Germ Theory and Lister's antiseptic method of surgery; in 1882 he reported on his experiment in which he observed a 'myriad of minute moving particles' and how carbolic spray had 'stopped all movement of the particles'.[22]

Later in 1884, Franks operated on two cases of obstruction of the small intestine, paving the way for the development of expertise in abdominal surgery at the hospital.

Training Institution for Protestant Nurses

The system of scientific medicine to which Dr Duncan was referring was creating a pressing demand for skilled nursing, a demand that could no longer be met by untrained and mostly uneducated nurses, and it was for this reason that hospital nurse training schemes were first established in Britain and Ireland in the 1860s and 1870s. The First Annual Report of 1858 included mention of plans for the training of nurses at the hospital: 'It is contemplated that the Adelaide Hospital will [establish] … a School in which Protestant Nurses may be trained.' The hospital's Managing Committee anticipated that 'Protestant women on proper recommendation' would be received from all parts of Ireland to the proposed new training school for nurses.[23] The plans to establish nurse training were further elaborated on with reference to Miss Bramwell, the newly-appointed Matron:

> [The Managing] Committee … have much pleasure in stating that they have been latterly encouraged and forwarded by the valuable aid gratuitously rendered by Miss Bramwell, an English Lady, who, with Miss Nightingale, had given herself to the care of our wounded soldiers in the Crimea. Her experience in regulating and superintending hospitals, and especially in training nurses, and directing nurse tending in general, it is trusted will be found most beneficial; and after some little time, and some further improvements, it is contemplated that the Adelaide Hospital will not only constitute a safe and happy retreat for our poor invalided brethren, but a School in which Protestant Nurses may be trained for external employment, or for the supply of other and similar establishments, so as to diffuse, as widely as possible, the essential benefits of the Institution.[24]

However, the second Annual Report for 1859 records that having 'rendered her services gratuitously', Miss Bramwell resigned as Matron, and the Managing Committee expressed its great appreciation to her for her 'kindness and attention to the patients, in ministering to their temporal and spiritual comfort.' Miss Bramwell's departure after only about eight months was somewhat forced and appears to have been related to disciplinary problems that she encountered.[25] In that year, Mrs Sarah Ruttle was appointed Matron on a salary of £50 per annum, and the Managing Committee came quickly to the view that 'after sufficient experience of Mrs Ruttle's capabilities, they feel bound to bear unqualified testimony to her energy and intelligence, as a valuable and efficient officer.' Under her 'judicious management', the Adelaide would soon be in a position 'to effect one of the main objects contemplated in this hospital; a training system for Protestant Nurses.'[26]

In the following year under Mrs Ruttle's 'untiring and judicious care and management', the newly re-opened Adelaide Hospital at Peter Street had 'been brought to a such a degree of order, combining all the benefits arising from the systematic arrangement with strict and unremitting attention to the comforts of the patients, as to render [it] ... second to none.'[27] In her careful superintendence she had brought cleanliness and good order to the hospital, and had given the assurance that the instructions of the physicians were carried out.[28] However, the extent to which nurse training was actually taking place in Mrs Ruttle's early years as Matron is somewhat unclear. In 1861, Mrs Ruttle travelled to Kaiserwerth in Germany to spend a month studying the system of nursing proffered by the deaconesses established under Pastor Theodor Fleidner, and she returned in September, after which time the Managing Committee reported that 'the Training Department for Nurses' had been recently opened under Mrs Ruttle's control.'[29] It is likely that small numbers of probationers were accepted for training after this time.

Proposals
In 1866, the Managing Committee considered two separate proposals for the founding of a nurse 'training establishment in connection with the hospital', and a Subcommittee was established to consider the matter. One scheme, devised by Mr Denis Crofton, proposed the provision of 'comfortable and healthful accommodation' for Matron and nurses, 'in the event of our Committee instituting a training establishment'. He estimated that a total annual cost of £200 would 'meet the necessary outlay involved by this experiment' and he recommended that 'it would be most desirable that the individuals to be trained as nurses should be taken from a superior class to that which now ordinarily furnishes persons of this description.' Proposed by Dr Walsh, the second scheme envisaged the renting of the old Molyneux Asylum at No 27 Peter St for the purpose of a 'training institution for nurses'. The institution would be separate from the hospital, but the nurses admitted to the institution would be trained in the wards of the hospital, under the 'sole control of the Matron ... and subject to all its regulations.' The Managing Committee ruled that Mr Crofton's proposal should have precedence. It also resolved that should a training institution be established, it should be for

'none but Protestant nurses' and that the services of one or more trained nurses 'of a superior class to those now employed in the hospital', should be engaged to undertake the training of the probationers in such an institution.[30]

The Subcommittee reported back in December 1866 that the plan to rent No 27 Peter Street for use as a training institution could not proceeded since the premises was not available for rent, that funds were not available to build premises on the grounds of the hospital, and that it was not possible to obtain a trained nurse from an English institution.[31] The Managing Committee resolved that it was desirable that a nurse should be trained in the Adelaide, 'become ultimately the head nurse under Mrs Ruttle' and undertake the training of probationers as soon as she became qualified. In February 1867, two nurses, Mrs Ward and Mrs Anderson, were admitted for training on a salary of one pound per month.

The Annual Report for 1867 refers to the fact that a 'Nurses' Training Establishment' in connection with the Hospital was 'set in foot in 1866', and had 'proved so successful, and the services of the trained nurses have been so much appreciated, and are in so great request, that it has been resolved to increase the number of nurses in the Training Institution.'[32] The Managing Committee was pleased that the Training Institution for Protestant Nurses, which the hospital 'was first to inaugurate [in Dublin]', had worked most successfully. The Medical Board also agreed that it had 'worked most satisfactorily', but was concerned that the demand for trained nurses was now greater than the numbers available. While the limited nurses' accommodation had restricted the number of nurses that could be trained, it was hoped that this difficulty would be shortly overcome so that Protestant families might at all times be able to 'obtain trained nurses of approved character and skill in the performance of their duties.'[33]

For some time after 1867, the training school was referred to as 'the Training Institution' or 'the training establishment connected with the hospital', and despite the plans to recruit additional nurses, the numbers recruited were small at that time. For example, in January 1868, just two nurses were admitted for training, and in December, a further two were admitted. In the period up to Mrs Ruttle's retirement, this was the pattern of recruitment, with just one or two nurses being admitted for training at any one time.

At the time, the need to train additional Protestant nurses was seen to be especially great in the face of the perceived threat of proselytising on the part of Catholic nursing sisters, 'whose dangerous influences [were] exercised upon many ill-informed Protestants.'[34] The bedside of sick Protestants in their own homes was seen as a place where such influences could be wielded, and the training of additional Protestant nurses for the Protestant public was viewed as an urgent need in countering such influences. As well as being a 'boon' to Protestant families, nurse training would also be an important source of income for the hospital.

By 1870, Adelaide-trained nurses were enhancing the hospital's public reputation and had 'given every satisfaction.'[35] In that year, the hospital's finances were in a 'favourable state', due largely to donations and bequests, and the hospital considered building additional accommodation, including clinical departments and additional accommodation for nurses. Although faced with the problem of limited nurses' accommodation, the hospital sought to increase the number of trained nurses, but it experienced difficulty in obtaining 'suitable persons to undergo the necessary probation', and urged Protestant clergymen to communicate the names of suitable persons to Mrs Ruttle. Although conducted 'on a limited scale' in the early 1870s, the training of nurses continued to be a source of satisfaction to the hospital authorities, due to the great material benefits derived from trained nurses tending to private cases, and because Adelaide nurses were now eagerly sought for private service.[36]

Mrs Lucinda Sullivan

In 1872 Mrs Ruttle resigned as Matron and Mrs Fegan was appointed Matron. However, Mrs Lucinda Sullivan was also appointed as Lady Superintendent at the same time, and with her appointment, Mrs Fegan did not carry the same authority as her predecessor. Instead she was most probably responsible for aspects of managing the hospital household, such as the kitchen and laundry, and the supervision of ward maids and other female servants. This is borne out in the fact that the Annual Report for 1874 records Mrs Fegan as Housekeeper and not as Matron.

Appointed in 1872, Mrs Lucinda Sullivan was the first person to hold the title 'Lady Superintendent' at the Adelaide Hospital. Mrs Sullivan's appointment coincided with the establishment of similar positions in other institutions at that time, most notably in the elite London voluntary hospitals, and as Lady Superintendent, she was responsible for the 'nursing and general superintendence of the Hospital.'[37] She was among the first of the corps of new lady superintendents of nursing that emerged in the period after the Nightingale School opened at St Thomas's Hospital in 1860, and like her contemporaries, she was an educated gentlewomen of the liberal Protestant middle-class community who possessed a strong desire to do philanthropic deeds and public service.[38] Like Florence Nightingale, and Sarah Ruttle,

Lucinda Sullivan attended the Kaiserwerth Institution in Germany for her formative nursing experience.

Although her time as Lady Superintendent at the Adelaide was relatively brief, Lucinda Sullivan was evidently of the same calibre of gentlewomen who possessed great organisational acumen and managerial deftness. The Managing Committee was quick to recognise that Mrs Sullivan's appointment had 'materially increased the comfort of the sick poor [in the hospital]', and early in her tenure as Lady Superintendent, the Nurse Training Department started by Mrs Ruttle, seemed to prosper, and move to a level of greater activity, particularly during 1873. The increases in fees earned by trained out-nurses was one of the few areas in which income for the hospital was increasing, and along with her 'admirable staff of lady nurses', her efforts contributed to the successful development of the hospital at that time. The lady nurses were praised for 'their warm sympathetic kindness and unpurchased services', and were greatly appreciated by the medical staff for their 'invaluable' assistance, and by the patients who experienced 'such great advantage' from their skilled nursing.[39] The Medical Board's Honorary Secretary Lombe Atthill reported on the changes in the Nursing Department which had taken place in that year under Mrs Sullivan:

> Mrs Sullivan has brought to the discharge of the duties she has so generously undertaken, energy, enthusiasm, knowledge, and judgment of no common kind. Those whose services she has secured as her assistants have, as a general rule, proved themselves singularly fitted for the work to which they have devoted themselves. An amount of careful attention has been given to individual cases, such as is rarely possible in a public institution; and we are convinced that during the past year several persons have been restored to health, whose lives, as far as we can judge, must have been lost, but for the assiduous and intelligent nursing which they received.[40]

Although receipts for out-nursing services showed a fall to £98 in 1874, the nurse training arrangements and the out-nursing services generally prospered, and the lady nurses continued to be the subject of praise from the Medical Board for having 'tended greatly' to the comfort of the sick and the success of medical treatments. However, in the glow of the growing success of the Nursing Department, in late 1874 Mrs Sullivan was obliged to resign her position as Lady Superintendent owing to poor health. Her unexpected and unplanned departure was a great blow to the hospital at the time, both in relation to the cause of her departure – she had succumbed to the effects of a cancer illness – and in the fact that she had given such valuable services to the hospital. During her relatively short tenure as Lady Superintendent, she had presided over what was acknowledged to have been a 'marked improvement' in several departments of the hospital, and she had contributed to the planning of the new Fever Wing at the hospital, which was eventually completed in 1877.

Aside from her role as Lady Superintendent at the Adelaide, Lucinda Sullivan is best remembered as a social reformer and for her great philanthropic work in founding the Cripples' Home in Bray. The daughter of Captain Brady, a British Army officer of the 2nd West India Regiment, she was married to Dr Robert Sullivan, a publisher and academic, but became a widow at age twenty eight after only three years of marriage. Following her husband's death she travelled to Germany and Switzerland, and while there, was involved in a near-fatal ferry accident on the Lake of Zurich in which two ferries sank. This life-changing event caused her to devote her life 'to the alleviation of human suffering' and in her diary she wrote: 'I saw then how God was calling me to give my life to his service and had saved me from a terrible end for that purpose!'[41]

Lucinda Sullivan was also an accomplished artist – she painted in oils, a medium not generally used by women at that time – and was a prolific writer in the mould of accomplished Victorian gentlewomen, writing on topics as varied as women's charity, women's temperance associations, and 'hospital work and lady nurses'. In her diary published in 1873, she wrote extensively of her experience of the ferry accident, and she also revealed her interest in nursing and in charitable work among the poor.[42] Having seen the work of 'the daughters of Germany [who] relieve the wants of the suffering body and minister the wants of the perishing soul,' she wrote: 'my deepest interest has been awakened on the subject of associated female workers among the sick, the ignorant, and the poor.' She anticipated engaging that interest by attending the Deaconesses' Houses 'to see for myself if I cannot learn something which may be turned to use in my own dear home [country].' Revealing the strong Christian basis of female philanthropy of the period, she concluded her diary with the entry: 'The way has all been made plain. A higher hand than mine has drawn out the plan.'

Lucinda's belief in the importance of Christian charity as the way of salvation for both the individual and society was expressed in her exhortation to the Young Women's Christian Association, of which she was President, to 'never lose sight of … the *power* of work, the *way* of work, and the *end* for which work is.'[43] With experience gained at the Deaconesses Institution at

Kaiserwerth, she worked for some time in a number of hospitals in Germany and Switzerland, and prior to her appointment at the Adelaide Hospital, worked at the Mildmay Deaconess Home in London. On her return to Dublin to take up her appointment at the Adelaide, she quickly turned her attention to the demands of her 'Christian duty' and to a particular concern of both Protestant and Catholic social reformers of the period, that of the welfare of children.[44] Driven by her strong commitment to social reform, she began to plan a home for 'the little ones who pass their miserable lives drifting from one hospital to another till their suffering ends in death.' Her plan was to combine 'hospital care, school training [and] industrial occupation ... in a pleasant country home', and through charitable fundraising, she acquired the former Workingmen's Club at Dargle Road in Bray and opened the Cripples' Home there in 1874. Like the 'energy, enthusiasm, knowledge, and judgment' that she brought to the running the Adelaide Hospital, she was thorough and energetic in setting up and running the Cripples' Home; as Maria Luddy writes: 'Sullivan's charitable enterprise was not undertaken lightly and she prepared herself thoroughly for the organisation, management, [and] efficient running of the home and the care of its inmates.'[45] The new Home greatly impressed Mr Gladstone, the Prime Minister of the day, who paid an unexpected visit in 1877 while staying at the nearby home of Lord Powerscourt. Mrs Gladstone also visited some days later and remarked in the visitors' book: 'I have not been disappointed.'[46]

Lucinda Sullivan died on 23 August 1881 at the age of 50 at the Bray Home, which she had founded some few short years previously. On her death, her sister Louise A. Brady carried on her work of running the home. Today Lucinda Sullivan's legacy lives on in the Sunbeam House Services that provide training, employment, support, and residential services for adults with an intellectual disability in South Dublin and throughout East Wicklow.

Plans

Mrs Sullivan's assistant Miss Reynolds was appointed her successor in early 1875, and the Medical Board expressed similar confidence in the ability of Miss Reynolds, whom it considered 'eminently fit ... to discharge with success the onerous duties of the post [of Lady Superintendent].'[47] At that time the growing demands for trained nurses for private cases and the important contribution that their fees were making to the income of the hospital – in 1875 these realised the sum of £241 – convinced the Managing Committee to include plans for new nurses' accommodation, when an extension to the

Hospital was being planned. The plans for the building of the new accommodation that would provide 'all the modern improvements which experience has demonstrated to be advantageous in the treatment of disease,' included provision for a fever hospital, surgical wards, operating theatre, wards for special cases, and accommodation for nurses.[48]

The plans for the extension of the hospital were greatly advanced in 1876 when the hospital purchased numbers 22 and 23 Peter Street and three houses in Wood Street, and by 1877, a greatly enlarged hospital was emerging. When complete, the new extension, named the Madeleine Wing, was a large three storey building to the side of the main building, incorporating a new operating theatre, and adding an additional twenty-five beds. The new Everina Wing for pay wards was attached to the side of the Madeleine Wing, and a new Fever Hospital was also completed on the site of the old fever sheds at Wood Street. Within twenty years of its reopening, the Adelaide Hospital had truly grown out of its 'chrysalis condition', and it was now a moderately-sized city centre hospital with its distinct facade at the corner of Peter Street and Peter's Row.

CHAPTER TWO

Nursing reform and the Adelaide Hospital, 1878-1888

Known as the 'Dublin School', the nineteenth-century movement in medical science lead to many new discoveries in pathology, medicine and surgery that advanced the treatment of diseases and reduced the pain and mortality associated with surgical operations. The rapid advances in medical science gave impetus to the development of a new system of modern nursing in Ireland, and the Adelaide School, established in 1859, was one of the earliest examples of this new system.

In 1877, the Adelaide Hospital was taking measures to improve its nursing arrangements through the provision of a new nurses' home to replace the 'deplorably insufficient' accommodation, which was described as unfit for 'responsible and hardly-worked women'.[1] At the ceremony to lay the corner stone for the new nurses' home in December 1877, much attention was paid to the pressing need for the training of skilled lady nurses, and the Rev Dr Maurice Neligan, a member of the Hospital Managing Committee, expressed the view that in matters of nursing, England was 'half a century before the Irish', and he called on 'the ladies of Dublin ... [to] throw themselves into their nursing work ... [since] it was not alone their duty but their privilege to help such work.'[2] While the Adelaide had done a great deal to provide a training school for nurses in Dublin, he believed that there was a great deal more that could be done, and he believed that ladies were 'very valuable as nurses', since they 'gave a tone to the nurses of poorer station'.

The Rev Neligan's call for more 'ladies' to take up nursing reflected the belief in Dublin and elsewhere at that time that hospitals needed to attract a better class of woman into nursing and that such women should be provided with a systematic training and 'such accommodation as either befitted their work or their position'. At the time, moves were in hand to achieve what would become a major transformation in the nursing arrangements across all of the Dublin hospitals.

Reforming hospital nursing in Dublin
In the 1870s, few nurses in Dublin were properly trained, and most nurses employed in the Dublin hospitals were recruited from the urban poor popul-

ation.[3] Described as 'nurses of poor station', many were older women who had received little formal education, and most entered employment as hospital nurses with no special instruction in the theory and practice of sick nursing. The idea that sick nursing was a special area of work that required special knowledge and skills and special training was not widely accepted in the middle of the nineteenth century. French Catholic nuns and German Protestant deaconesses had well developed systems of sick nursing in the early nineteenth century – Napoleon went to battle with his corps of Catholic military nurses – and the system of nursing proffered by the Irish Sisters of Mercy who attended the sick and wounded soldiers in the Crimean War during the 1850s was based on well tried ideas about the most effective means of treating fevers, pain and wounds. However, the skilled nursing provided by religious sisters was developed through practical experience, and not through systematic theoretical and technical training. For the Sisters of Mercy and other religious sisterhoods, skilled nursing required a moral sense rather than scientific training. The idea of a systematic training in nursing had only gained wider acceptance after the Crimean War, and it was based on a combination of technical training, and also the moral sense that Nightingale so much admired in the work of the German deaconesses.[4] The introduction of new nurse training schemes, into which younger middle-class women were recruited, represented the major element of nursing reform and introduced modern nursing.

The establishment of systematic training for nurses was driven by advances in medical science, including advances in understandings of infection and the role of sanitation in preventing contagion. The reform of nursing was also part of the reform of hospitals and other public institutions; in the case of voluntary hospitals this involved new methods of hospital management, the introduction of better construction, improved sanitation, improved dietary for patients and staff, and better living arrangements for staff. Nursing and sanitary reform were also part of wider social reform movements that included reforms in education, child welfare, and public health. To social reformers of the time, the conditions of the sick poor, including poverty, poor sanitation, diseases, and alcohol misuse, were as much related to the poor moral character of the poorer classes as to their actual condition of poverty. Many social reformers were educated middle-class women whose public philanthropic work was challenging the expectation that the 'lady' should confine herself to domestic affairs.[5]

While it is likely that many untrained hospital nurses provided good nursing care, their limited education and lack of formal training made them increasingly incapable of working effectively in the new era of hospital scientific medicine, and in particular, of meeting the needs of patients who were now undergoing ever more complex medical and surgical treatments.[6] Most of the hospital matrons of the period, who had overall responsibility for nursing and the hospital household, were themselves untrained in sick nursing. The case for reforming nursing was also strong in the face of the numerous reports emanating from the Dublin hospitals and concerning poor nursing care, improper conduct, neglect of duty, and poor ward sanitation. These reports included accounts of nurses' 'gross impropriety of conduct' and 'drunkenness and incapacity', and accounts of patients' 'dirty hands and faces' and hospital wards being 'in a shocking state.'[7] On a visit to Sir Patrick Dun's Hospital as late as in 1878, one social reformer reported that she found two night nurses to be 'ignorant, inefficient women, who can neither read nor write'.[8]

There were moves to reform hospital nursing through the introduction of proper training for nurses as early as 1859 when, following the reopening of the Adelaide Hospital at Peter Street, the hospital authorities had as one of its 'main objects' the establishment of 'a training system for Protestant Nurses.' Sarah Ruttle was appointed Matron in that year, and in 1861 attended the Deaconess Institution in Kaiserwerth for a period of one month to study the system of nursing there.[9]

The Institution at Kaiserwerth was founded in 1836 by Theodor Fleidner, a Lutheran clergyman, with the assistance of his wife Fredericke, as a religious foundation to give relief to the poor and to train women of good character as deaconesses.[10] It developed a reputation across Europe and beyond in the nineteenth century for its work in caring for the sick and for training women in sick nursing. Sarah Ruttle was one among many ladies to visit the Institution. Florence Nightingale and Elizabeth Fry were also visitors, and it is likely that they were drawn to the Institution because of its international reputation and because its emphasis on Christian charity accorded with their deeply held religious beliefs. It was also for many years one of the few examples of a place in which women were systematically trained in the care of the sick. The fact that it was a Protestant institution was also significant in explaining why Sarah Ruttle and Lucinda Sullivan attended. The influence of the Kaiserwerth Institution on the development of modern nursing cannot be overstated, particularly given Nightingale's connection with the Institution.

Very serious defects: the Dublin Hospital Sunday Fund

By the end of the 1860s, the Adelaide Hospital 'Training Department' had produced many fully trained nurses and had proved 'a great success'. However, while nurse training was being conducted under Mrs Sullivan up to 1874, it appears that in 1879 'no systematic training' was being conducted at the hospital under her successor Miss Reynolds.

Along with the Adelaide Hospital, the only other nurse training scheme in operation in Dublin in the 1860s and 1870s was that which the Dublin Nurses' Training Institution at No 4 Holles Street provided. Established sometime after 1860 as an independent institution for the training of Protestant nurses by Archbishop Trench, the Institution had arrangements with Dr Steevens' and Sir Patrick Dun's hospitals for the training of probationers.[11] Aside from these arrangements, no system for the training of nurses existed in the Dublin voluntary hospitals, which continued to recruit nurses from the poorer classes. This situation was a cause of increasing concern to social reformers and to the members of the boards of management of the Dublin hospitals during the 1870s. The impetus for a more wholesale reform of hospital nursing came from a charitable body, the Dublin Hospital Sunday Fund.[12]

The Dublin Hospital Sunday Fund was founded in 1874 as a fundraising movement for voluntary hospitals.[13] The founders of the Fund included members of the Dublin aristocracy, businessmen, medical men, and clergymen, and its patron was the Lord Lieutenant of Ireland. Significantly, some of its members, including the Earl of Meath, were members of the boards of Dublin hospitals.[14] Through the annual 'Hospital Sunday' collection at participating churches, the Dublin Hospital Sunday Fund raised relatively large sums of money for the Dublin Protestant hospitals. In its first year the Fund generated £3,619 and it quickly became an important source of income for the hospitals. Having debated the subject for a number of years, in 1876 the Adelaide Hospital decided to join the Fund, and in its first year of membership, the hospital's share of the Fund was £765.4s. In 1877, the Fund donated a total of £622.1.9 to the hospital, the largest sum donated by the Fund in that year.

By giving large monetary grants on an annual basis to the Dublin hospitals, the Fund's Executive Council saw that its control over funds was a way of achieving reforms in hospital management, and it believed that since it contributed nearly £4,000 a year to the hospitals, it was 'bound to have regard to the efficiency of the arrangements for the care of the patients in these institutions'.[15] On these grounds, the Executive Council established a

Committee on Nursing in 1878 'to inquire into the arrangements for Nursing in each of the hospitals participating in the Hospital Sunday Fund'. The Committee on Nursing of eleven members undertook visits of inspection to fourteen Dublin hospitals and in 1879 published 'a valuable and detailed report' on the nursing arrangements in the hospitals.[16]

The Dublin Hospital Sunday Fund's Committee on Nursing Report contained detailed descriptions of the arrangements for nurse training, nurses' conditions of employment, and the arrangements for the efficient nursing of patients, including the layout of hospital wards.[17] The Committee on Nursing found that, excluding the training which Sir Patrick Dun's provided in association with the Training Institution at Holles Street, there were 'no establishments for the systematic training of nurses' at any of the Dublin hospitals.[18] While there was an 'arrangement at the Adelaide for probationers', the Committee reported that there did not seem to be 'any systematic training carried out at that hospital'.

Only at Sir Patrick Dun's, St. Mark's and Cork Street hospitals were nurses 'directly controlled by trained superintendents' and in seven hospitals, among them Dr Steevens', the Meath, and the Adelaide, the nursing arrangements were found to be 'under the control of persons who have never had any special training for their duties.'[19] Another 'very serious defect' in the Dublin hospitals was the custom of combing the duties of nurse and ward maid, meaning that persons so employed 'must be drawn from a lower social class than that from which nurses should be derived'. Poor wages and defective sleeping, cooking and eating arrangements were also reported, and nurses were 'over-worked, partly from defective method, and partly from want of sufficient relaxation, air and exercise.' The Committee also reported 'the want of proper codes of printed rules' for nurses.

In making recommendations, the Committee on Nursing wrote that it was essential to good hospital nursing that the person in control of nurses should herself be a trained nurse; each hospital should have a lady superintendent, 'fully capable of carrying out hospital nursing in all its details, and of giving systematic instruction to those who may be placed under her.'[20] In its Report, the Committee wrote that it was 'the duty of hospital authorities ... to take their part in training nurses' and provide nurses with better accommodation, better pay, daily relaxation, and periodic holidays. In the Committee's view, the whole system of nursing could not be reformed until 'a better class of nurse' was employed.

The Committee on Nursing Report gave an unflattering picture of conditions for both patients and nurses in some of Dublin's most prominent hospitals, and in order to ensure that its recommendations for reform would be carried out, the Committee linked the grants awarded by the Dublin Hospital Sunday Fund to the extent of reform undertaken by each hospital.[21] A hospital participating in the Fund would in future have to earn its contribution from the Fund, by demonstrating that it had undertaken 'such reforms as the managers of the [Sunday] Fund may suggest.'[22] The Committee hoped that the hospital authorities would 'do their best ... to carry out any recommendations, which may be adopted by the [Fund].' A copy of the Report was sent to the fourteen hospitals inspected and hospital managers were asked to 'pay special attention to the [Report's] recommendations', and give a written response to the Report.[23] Since financial income and reputations were at stake, the hospitals responded quickly, and most took measures to introduce the sort of nursing reforms that the Report called for.

The Adelaide responds

Shortly before the deputation from the Committee on Nursing made its visit of inspection to the Adelaide Hospital, the Adelaide Medical Board wrote to the Managing Committee stating that 'in their opinion, the nursing of the hospital is not in as satisfactory a state as they could wish', and requested the Managing Committee to 'institute enquiries as to the best means of rendering more efficient both the nursing of the hospital and the training of private nurses.'[24] When the deputation visited the Adelaide on 19 December 1878, it found that while the Adelaide employed probationers who assisted the trained nurses, there were a number of defects in the nursing arrangements:

> There was a Superintendent of Nurses, but she had had no systematic training for her special duties ... Although there was an arrangement for probationers, no systematic training was carried out ... Hours of sleep seemed adequate, but times for sleeping were variable. No facilities for recreation or rest were provided in the hospital. The nurses could 'go out' for 3 to 4 hours twice a week.[25]

Why the training of nurses should have faltered in 1878 is most likely due a number of factors. Mrs Sullivan's untimely departure in 1874 had left a great deficit in the Nursing Department that Miss Reynolds could not make up. Mrs Sullivan had come to the Adelaide with the experience of her time at the Kaiserwerth Institution and with considerable experience of hospital management, while it appears that Miss Reynolds had no formal training in nursing or hospital management. In addition, the more practical problem of the 'deplorably insufficient' nurses' accommodation restricted the means for recruiting and training nurses. When the Committee on Nursing inspected the Adelaide in late 1878, it is evident that the hospital was already taking steps to re-establish nurse training; it was building new nurses' accommodation and had also established an internal committee to examine the hospital's nursing arrangements. That the Adelaide should receive a negative report from the Committee on Nursing was more the result of bad timing and less any deliberate policy on the part of the hospital not to recruit and train lady nurses. However, soon after the visit by the Nursing Committee, as will be seen presently, the hospital was forced to curtail the recruitment and training of nurses due to severe financial difficulties.

Miss Reynolds

Soon after its visit to the Adelaide, the Committee on Nursing wrote to the Adelaide authorities in early January 1879, asking them to provide it with its proposal to address any defective arrangements contained in the Committee's Report. The Managing Committee responded, advising that it had taken steps to improve the nursing arrangements.[26] These steps included the adoption of a code of rules for the nursing organisation of the hospital, which providing for a Lady Superintendent and four divisional lady nurses. The Lady Superintendent would have 'full authority' and be responsible for 'proper discipline and carrying out the rules connected with the Nursing Department.'[27] While not 'a certificated trained nurse', the Lady Superintendent Miss Reynolds had gained experience under the supervision of her predecessor Mrs Sullivan. However, in June 1880, in response to the specific recommendation of the Committee on Nursing 'that the person in control of nurses should herself be a trained nurse', the Managing Committee resolved to send Miss Reynolds to London to take a course in nurse training and hospital management. This was so that she might 'become experientially acquainted with the details of the newest and best system of hospital management ... with the view to the special improvement of the nursing staff, as also of the general management of the [Adelaide] Institution.'[28]

Miss Reynolds secured a place at St Bartholomew's Hospital and in November left for a period of six months, during which time no new lady probationers would be received. During her absence, Miss Lindsay of St Patrick's Home for Nurses for the Sick Poor was appointed as acting Lady Superintendent.[29] Also on a recommendation of the Committee on Nursing, the Managing Committee undertook to subdivide the hospital wards for the purpose of classification of diseases and this would necessitate the employment of additional nurses.

Miss Reynolds evidently impressed her London hosts; in December Mrs Machin, the Lady Superintendent at St Bartholomew's, wrote to the Managing Committee of the Adelaide, advising that she was 'much pleased' with Miss Reynolds, who had 'entered so heartily into the spirit of the work and is evidently not easily overcome by difficulties'. Mrs Machin also wrote that it was a pleasure 'to put her in the way of getting any advantage there is to be had here' and she remarked that 'in somethings, I fancy that the Adelaide Hospital is much more modern than this one.' When Miss Reynolds returned in May 1881, the Managing Committee expressed its deep gratitude to Miss Lindsay for her 'great ability, tact, discretion, and zeal … while in charge of the hospital.'[30] Following Miss Reynolds' return to Dublin, Mrs Machin again wrote to the Managing Committee, remarking that Miss Reynolds had been 'indefatigable in the discharge of the duties committed to her'. She was 'highly capable of directing those less experienced, and with an earnestness and conscientiousness that must always tend to promote and maintain a high tone of morality among those coming under her influence.'

Changes

The Rules for Nurses, which were revised in June 1880 and which were to be displayed 'in a conspicuous part of each of the hospital wards', included the provisions that probationers were allowed 'one evening on the week [only] and on all other evenings … they are not to be absent from the hospital after five o'clock', and nurses going out between 2 and 5 o'clock in the afternoon should obtain the permission of the Lady Superintendent. Nurses and probationers were expected to attend Sunday service and evening prayer in the boardroom, and a book of attendance at Divine Service was to be kept. In communicating the rules to Miss Reynolds, the Secretary of the Managing Committee remarked:

> In receiving these Ladies into the Hospital on the basis of the Rules, I would remind you that you as Lady Superintendent, and the Committee are responsible to the parents and friends of these Ladies, [and] that these rules which are framed in their interests are to be obeyed.[31]

A feature of the nursing reforms that took place in most Dublin hospitals following the Report of the Committee on Nursing was the many enforced resignations, particularly of older untrained nurses and ward maids.[32] In 1879, the services of Nurse Kennedy were discontinued as she was 'unfit to become a ward nurse', and as she had given 'long and faithful services' to the Adelaide, it is probable that Nurse Kennedy was an untrained nurse. Later in February 1881, with her salary paid one month in advance, a ward maid was 'at once parted with.'

Despite severe financial difficulties that restricted the number of nurses that could be employed, the training of probationers was occurring soon after the visit of the Committee on Nursing; in November 1880, three probationers, Stonex, Parkes, and McClean were examined. Reporting to the Managing Committee on the three nurses' performance in the examination, the examiners Walter G. Smith, R. Dancer Purefoy and Kendal Franks remarked:

> In the surgical and obstetrical parts of the examination we report that the answering was exceptionally good ... In the medical part of the examination the answering was good, but all the nurses were deficient in the knowledge of acute febrile diseases. The Examiners ... advise that ... no probationer for the future be certified as a thoroughly trained nurse, who has not received at least three months' training in the Fever House.'[33]

The examiners concluded their report with a strong recommendation that the services of all three nurses be retained by the hospital. By this time, the Managing Committee recognised that by training its own probationers, it would not only secure a supply of fully trained nurses to meet its needs, but it would also have the assurance of 'knowing the capabilities of each nurse prior to her being entrusted with the care of the patients'.[34]

While the introduction of the reforms recommended by the Committee on Nursing represented an initial financial burden for the hospitals, particularly through the added costs of improved wages and better living accommodation, the investment would be rewarded when properly trained and certified nurses could earn substantial monies for the hospitals through the nursing of private cases. For the Adelaide, these earning were substantial in the decades after 1880. Of more immediate benefit were the great improvements in the quality of sick nursing and hospital sanitation, and the reforms also provided nurses with the sort of skills seen as necessary to support the range of medical and surgical treatments that were being developed at the time.

'A very serious state of things'

The visit of the Dublin Hospital Sunday Fund's Committee on Nursing to the Adelaide Hospital coincided with the completion of building work to 'introduce the most recent improvements in hospital construction in con-nection with ventilation and sanitary arrangements.'[35] When completed in October 1879, the work had provided the new Fever House, the new Madeline Wing containing a new operating theatre, alterations to the dis-pensary, and new accommodation for nurses. The addition of the operating theatre was especially welcomed, and in 1879 the Medical Board attributed the low mortality rate associated with surgical operations performed in that year to 'the excellent sanitary condition of the hospital and to the rigid adher-ence to cleanliness in the management of [surgical] cases'.[36]

The building work had resulted in an effective doubling of the size of the hospital, and with it a 'much larger expenditure than was at first contem-plated', with much of the expenditure going on accommodation for nurses.[37] The additional cost of the 'improved and extended system of nursing' resulted in much added expense on the hospital. Although costly, the Managing Committee agreed that 'this important branch of work is more appreciated than heretofore and ... [the] increases in the staff of trained nurses, which the new building will admit to, is much required.'[38] However, the high financial burden of the new buildings was greatly added to at the time by a 'serious financial loss ... sustained through the ingenuous and gross mal-practices of the late Registrar, Mr James Franklin.' While he produced 'most satisfactory' references when first appointed in 1875, Mr Franklin absconded, having 'appropriated for his own use the sum of £735.5s.9d.'

Rigid economy
With the addition of the Fever Wing, there were now 'two distinct hospitals ... to be maintained,' and the hospital found itself in severe financial diffi-culties with a large overdraft. The Managing Committee resolved that 'whereas the income of the hospital had not increased in proportion (if at all) to the development of the hospital accommodation ... the present system of nursing be modified, the lady nurses or some of them be dispensed with, and a more economic system adopted [and] ... that a thorough revision of the general arrangements of the hospital, including food, fuel and lighting be made with a view to rigid economy.'[39] The plan to remedy the situation by dismissing nurses would risk putting off the time when the hospital could be fully compliant with the recommendations of the Committee on Nursing.

At the time the accounts showed an overdraft of between two and three thousand pounds, a situation that presented a real threat of closure of the entire hospital. Faced with this threat, in February 1880, the Managing Committee decided to close five wards – two operation wards, the male and female eye wards and the ward for diseases of women – and to dispense with the services of the divisional nurses in these wards. The total complement of nurses in the main building was also reduced to twelve and in the Fever Wing to just two, and the Managing Committee dispensed with the services of all nurses and probationers in excess of these numbers. No free patients would be admitted after 1st March 1880, except in urgent need of treatment, and the fees for pay wards were set at between ten shillings and £2. While the Nursing Department was severely affected by the financial crisis, no response was forthcoming from the Medical Board as to how it might assist in curtailing expenses. In the event, the Managing Committee decided to withhold payment of medical men's expenses other than their salaries.

The Annual General Meeting of April 1880 discussed the 'very serious state of things', which necessitated a temporary reduction in the number of intern patients.[40] The hospital was in such a parlous financial state that in May the Managing Committee resolved that 'no lady nurses or lady probationers in future be appointed and that the present lady nurses and lady probationers be at the expiration of their term discontinued.' This resolution clearly alarmed the members of the Medical Board in attendance, and doctors Barton and Richardson put down a motion 'that the Medical Board be requested to give their opinion … upon the advisability or non-advisability of continuing the lady nursing [system] in this hospital.'[41] The opinion of the Medical Board was presented at the next meeting of the Managing Committee in June:

> The Medical Board are of the opinion that the supervision of trained lady nurses is of great value in maintaining the efficient nursing of the patients and the cleanliness of the wards, and that if young women are to be trained in the hospitals as nurses in private families, the presence of one or more such trained lady nurses is indispensable.[42]

This view was formally adopted as a resolution of the Medical Board. The resolution of the Managing Committee not to appoint lady nurses and lady probationers in the future was lost to what was a compromise resolution, which amended the Nurses' Rules to the effect that 'no lady nurses or lady probationers be received under 30 years of age.' In the event, appointments of probationers were postponed. With its counter motion, the Medical Board had effectively saved the system of lady nursing at that time.

At the same time, the hospital issued an appeal through the national newspapers 'drawing attention to the wants of the hospital', and a second appeal was directed at all clergymen of the Irish Church asking for their 'kind assistance' in making appeals to their congregations for financial support. Despite some increases in income, by August 1880 the debt of the hospital was now well in excess of £4,000. Further measures to reduce costs were considered, including the closure of male and female wards on the west wing, the closure of two ten shilling pay wards, the temporary closure of the Fever House, and a 'proportional reduction' in the number of nurses. Giving details of the debts, the Honorary Secretary Mr Clarendon advised the Managing Committee that 'the very existence of the hospital depends upon their present action, for if the dept is not reduced, the hospital must be closed.' The proposed action would involve an almost total closure of the hospital, with provision for just thirty-five patients. In order to avoid such an extreme step, the Medical Board made alternative proposals, which included reductions in the salaries of the Registrar and Apothecary, and measures to reduce the costs of food and heating; gas heating would be turned down in the evenings and paraffin lamps would replace gas lighting.

With savings made on running costs and with increases in charitable donations, the extreme measures were modified, and sixty free beds, twenty pay beds, one apartment in the Fever House, and the pay wards were kept open. By December 1880, three new lady probationers were admitted and a 'visitation of fever' in the hospital in February 1881 necessitated the employment of additional nurses. While the financial difficulties persisted, by August 1881 the debt was reduced to £2,100, but remained a cause of 'the greatest anxiety' to the Managing Committee. The services of four nurses were dispensed with and the medical officers were requested to curtail the ordering of extra dietaries and to discharge any patents fit for discharge and any 'whose case had become chronic' – at the time the average length of stay was 30 days, a period far in excess of most other Dublin hospitals.[43] The commonest medical cases were those admitted with pulmonary consumption, and the Medical Board urged that such cases would be best treated in a consumptive hospital, 'in a healthy locality in the country near Dublin'.

A favourable state
The extreme cost-saving measures began to achieve results and later in 1881, while unpaid debt on the building work amounted to almost £4,500, income from donations, subscriptions, bequests and pay wards amounted to about £3,200, and the Managing Committee expressed the hope that it could soon increase the present number of nurses to meet the demands for private nursing. By February 1882, the number in training was six probationer nurses and one lady paying probationer, and four trained nurses were available for out

nursing. The grants awarded by the Dublin Hospital Sunday Fund contributed significantly to the debt reduction at that time; in 1882, the Fund awarded £835, and in 1883 it awarded £838.[44] These grants included 'the special bonus on account of improved nursing arrangements.' A bequest of £600 to provide 'a home for nurses when found to be overworked or requiring temporary repose' was also received around this time. The hospital had difficulty in finding a suitable location for the home and it would, in time, build a new nurses' home on the grounds of the hospital.

In 1883, the funds of the hospital were now 'in a favourable state', and it was possible to increase the wages of certified nurses to £20 per annum. Miss Reynolds's salary was increased to £100 and she and another nurse were granted leave to 'take lessons at Bray in the system of "massage" for restoring paralysed limbs'. It was also possible to re-designate a number of pay beds as free beds, and a Reserve Fund created from legacies was established. By 1884 the hospital had reopened all its wards for the receipt of patients. The income earned by trained out-nurses in that year was almost £300, and this source of income was limited only by the limited accommodation available for nurses.

With its improved financial circumstances, the hospital was now endeavouring to rebuild its nursing workforce, and despite the provision of new nurses' rooms in 1879 and the conversion of a ward for use as a temporary nurses' dormitory in 1884, the available accommodation was insufficient to meet the hospital's needs. A decision was taken to erect a new nurses' home on the grounds of the hospital on the site formerly occupied by the old Dispensary House, close to the Ledwich Medical School.[45] By the end of 1886, a new nurses' home, 'a most valuable and much needed adjunct to the hospital', along with apartments for the Lady Superintendent, had been completed at a cost of nearly £3,000. The home would offer all nurses 'when not occupied by their arduous and anxious duties elsewhere, a comfortable home in which they can enjoy the rest or privacy they require'.[46]

With the short-lived but severe financial crisis now behind it, the hospital could look forward to meeting its goal of providing medical relief for the sick Protestant poor of Ireland. By 1886, the hospital was back to full activity, and the number of major surgical operations performed in that year was 190; this number included amputations, removal of tumours, operations on bone, intestinal operations, and operations on the eye. Fevers and consumption accounted for a large number of the medical cases in that year. The hospital's Nursing Department, which was most severely affected by the financial crisis, could look forward to a brighter future, with additional nurses and probationers housed in the most modern accommodation.

CHAPTER THREE

'Hail spot cotton print': The Adelaide nurse, 1889-1899

While the establishment of the Adelaide Hospital Nursing School predated the widespread nursing reforms of the 1880s, the hospital participated in aspects of the reforms, including the provision of proper training for its Lady Superintendent and improvements in nurses' conditions of employment. Aside from the skilled professional service that fully trained and certified nurses were giving, private nursing service was becoming increasingly important as a source of income for the hospital. Although the Adelaide had its peculiar religious character, nurses' training experiences at the hospital in this period were typical of those of other Dublin hospitals.

The Nursing Committee

In 1888, all was not well in the Nursing Department when it appears that Miss Reynolds did not have the full confidence of some members of the Managing Committee. In January Miss Reynolds tendered her resignation, but she later withdrew it in March. In April the question of the superintendence of the hospital was brought before the Managing Committee and a motion was proposed by Lord Butler 'that in order to restore to ... the hospital that harmony, the absence of which has so seriously interfered with the satisfactory working of the Managing Committee, and which is caused altogether by differences with the Lady Superintendent, that a change should at once be made to the holder of the post.'[1] It appears that there was disharmony between Miss Reynolds and the Housekeeper, Miss Weirder, who had responsibility for the hospital household. When Miss Weirder tendered her resignation in April, Lord Butler, a member of the Managing Committee, expressed regret that she 'should have to leave the hospital for even a single day.'

In a compromise move, the Medical Board proposed that a person independent of the Lady Superintendent be appointed 'who will undertake the superintendence of the nurses' home and the training of nurses for the hospital and out-nursing.' However, it was feared that this proposal would bring much added financial burden that could not be justified, and the Managing Committee was split on the proposal. Both Lord Butler and Canon Neligan wished to see the Nursing Department constituted as a separate department from the Hospital Establishment in its finances, superintendence and management. A special Sub-committee was set up to examine the proposal and in June it recommended that the Nursing Establishment 'in its domestic arrangements, economy, and all details be entirely separate from the Hospital Establishment.'[2] The Nursing Establishment should be 'subject to the supervision of a Lady Superintendent ... thoroughly trained in a first class hospital', who would 'supervise [probationers] ... generally both when on and off duty ... arrange for their lectures ... arrange their hours for duty for meals and for recreation.' The Lady Superintendent would also be responsible for the comfort and welfare of the nurses, have charge of the nurses' home and preside over the meals of the nurses and probationers.' and she should 'be responsible for the making of the probationers' clothes and as far as possible shall utilise their leisure for this purpose.' She should also supply to the Lady Superintendent of the Hospital Establishment 'a list of all properly trained and qualified nurses for outpatients, with observations as to the class of cases, for which each nurse is especially suited.'

The disharmony that led to the proposal to separate the management of the nursing and hospital household departments was the catalyst for the establishment of a new Nursing Committee that would take overall control of all nursing arrangements at the hospital, and prepare the new rules governing the management of the separate departments.

The Nursing Committee would 'meet at least once a month to consider all matters connected with the Department ... [including] the working and financial state of the Nursing Department.'[3] The new Committee comprised six members, three medical men and three lay members, and it was empowered to co-opt any member of the recognised staff of the Hospital 'to afford the benefit of his experience or assistance'. Once established, the Committee considered all applications for probationership training, presided over all decisions concerning the Nursing Department, including appointments and dismissals, and took monthly reports from the Lady Superintendent.

Separate Superintendence

The Nursing Committee held its inaugural meeting on 8 October 1888, at which it was resolved to recommend to the Management Committee that 'immediate steps [be taken] to have a Lady Superintendent of the Nursing Department appointed.'[4] It requested Miss Reynolds to supply 'a full list of all the nurses belonging to the hospital ... with the dates of their appointment, the length of training of each in the Medical, Surgical and Fever

Wards, stating how many and which of them have passed the Medical Board Examinations, the salary now paid to each ... how each one is now occupied, together with such further observations as she may wish to make.'[5]

When the new Nursing Committee next met a week later, Miss Reynolds had supplied it with the information that it had requested, and the Committee wasted no time in drawing up plans for the reorganisation of the Nursing Department. These included the introduction of 'separate superintendence' over the hospital, whereby the Matron would be responsible for the hospital household, including the general upkeep and cleanliness of the clinical departments, and the Superintendent of Nurses would have responsibility for all matters relating to nursing, including the recruitment and training of probationers.[6]

In 1888, having served the hospital for fourteen years, Miss Reynolds retired 'on account of failing health'. At her retirement, she was praised for her 'indefatigable energy, her personal merits, her extended influence, her general courtesy, and her uniform kindness to the patients and the subordinate staff', and she was presented with a clock and a purse of sovereigns.[7] The posts of Lady Superintendent and Matron were advertised. Henrietta C. Poole, the 'unanimous choice' from among five ladies who were interviewed, was appointed Lady Superintendent in October 1888. Like Miss Reynolds, Miss Poole trained at St Bartholomew's Hospital in London, and her appointment was mentioned in *The Nursing Record*:

> Miss Henrietta Poole has been appointed Superintendent of Nursing at the large and important Adelaide Hospital in Dublin ... and being a native of the Emerald Isle, will probably be the better able to enlist the co-operation of her countrywomen in the great work of organising a system of modern nursing, which she will have to carry out.[8]

Following interviews for the post of Matron, the Nursing Committee confirmed the appointment of Gertrude Knight in December 1888. Miss Knight had been a ward sister at the Radcliffe Infirmary in Oxford, and at the time of her appointment was Matron of the nearby Dublin Eye and Ear Infirmary. With her appointment, the St Bartholomew's connection was further strengthened, since she too had trained there, having entered as a probationer in 1880. The appointment of Miss Knight was also noted in *The Nursing Record*, which congratulated the Adelaide on securing the services of Miss Knight who was 'no one more deserving of the highest rank'.[9] The additional cost of replacing Miss Reynolds with two ladies resulted in a merger of the post of Matron with that of Housekeeper. As Matron, Miss Knight would be assisted in her additional duties by a senior probationer 'who may desire to learn housekeeping'. At the time of the new appointments, draft Regulations for the Training of Nurses in the Adelaide Hospital were laid before the Nursing Committee and later approved, along with the draft application form for Probationers.

On her appointment Miss Poole was invited to 'draw up a tabular statement as to how she would propose to nurse the hospital – the position and the number of nurses, and the probable expense.'[10] Miss Poole quickly set about the work of preparing a plan for the Nursing Department, which she laid before the Nursing Committee in early November. Her plan included the proposal that 'four Divisional Nurses ... shall be appointed at a salary of £30 a year each [and] each Sister shall superintend a division and train the probationers under her.'[11] Probationers would complete three years of training, and having passed an examination at the end of the third year, would receive a certificate of training. Miss Poole also proposed that a nurse's engagement with the hospital should then cease and only those nurses who had 'proved themselves specially competent' should be retained. In the first year probationers would serve as 'ward probationers' at a salary of £6, in the second year they would act as 'ward nurses' at a salary of £9, and in the third year would be placed on the list for private nursing at a salary of £12. Miss Poole's proposals also indicated the total number of nurses required for the 'proper running of the hospital'; this was four sisters, ten second year nurses, and twelve first year probationers, with the total cost of salaries calculated to be £282. Information previously supplied by Miss Reynolds indicated that at that time a total complement of twenty four nurses, in training and qualified, was employed on 'regular duties' at a cost of £354 to the hospital.

At its meeting on 13 November the Managing Committee adopted the scheme for nursing as proposed by Miss Poole, and authorised her to select divisional nurses and supply their names and qualifications to the Nursing Committee. Miss Poole duly presented the names of two ladies, Miss Evans and Miss Sneyd, who were invited to attend with their papers before entering into any engagement with the hospital. In the following April, Evans, along with nurses Stevenson and Henderson had completed their probation as divisional nurses to the satisfaction of the Nursing Committee and were duly appointed, and a Miss Browne, who had the 'highest testimonials', was appointed Divisional Nurse to the Female Landing.

The work of reorganising the Nursing Department was continued by Miss Poole throughout 1889. This work involved the establishment of two main departments, 'one for the proper nursing of the patients in the hospital, the other for the supply of thoroughly trained and skilled nurses for patients in their own houses.'[12] Miss Poole took charge of the entire Nursing Department, while the Nursing Committee supervised its management, and early experience indicated that the new system of management had 'already shown to be excellent.' The new nursing arrangements were summarised at the time:

> For the purposes of nursing, the hospital is divided into four divisions – viz., male, female, children, and fever. Each of these is under the charge of a divisional nurse. Two of the divisional nurses now in the hospital are nurses who, by long service in the institution, and by their proved skill in nursing and in training probationers, the Nursing Committee considered had earned promotion, and who were therefore advanced by the Managing Committee to their present position; the other two divisional nurses have been trained in London hospitals, and were highly recommended to the Committee on account of their superior training, as well as their skill and devotion to their calling. The several wards in each division are placed under the charge of a staff nurse, who is again assisted by probationers.[13]

The Managing Committee was pleased with the arrangements, and expressed its thanks to Miss Poole 'for her management of the Nursing Department, as evidenced in the first place by its financial condition, and secondly by the manner in which the patients in the wards have been cared for', and the Committee also remarked on the 'high sense of the services here rendered by Miss Knight'. The Committee also expressed confidence that the friends and visitors of the hospital could be satisfied 'that they are instrumental in supporting a hospital which is a credit to the Protestants of Ireland, and which will compare favourably with any hospital in the United Kingdom.'[14]

In 1889, the number of beds opened for continuous use was 125. Once again, however, the hospital was experiencing severe financial difficulties at the time, and it was recommended that the number of beds in use be reduced to ninety five, that the number of nurses and probationers be reduced to fifteen, and that the wages of nurses be reduced. Out nurses should be deployed in the hospital when in the nurses' home, thereby making additional savings. However, the proposed reduction in the salaries of divisional nurses Henderson and Stevenson from £30 to £20 per annum alarmed the Medical Board, which warned that the hospital might lose their services. Their salaries were retained at the higher level, owing to 'the generosity of a Wm. Giggis.'

Henrietta Poole and Gertrude Knight

In 1894, Henrietta Poole left the Adelaide to take up an appointment as Matron of the East Lancashire Infirmary in Blackburn. Miss Poole was a member of the Royal British Nurses' Association (RBNA), the professional body founded in 1887 to campaign for professional regulation of nursing through state registration. In her role as a member of the Council of the RBNA, she actively campaigned on the issues of the day. When the RBNA admitted physicians and surgeons in 1892, opponents of state registration gained control of the Council, leading some of its founders to form a new professional association, the Matron's Council of Great Britain and Ireland.[15] The takeover by anti-registrationists angered Henrietta Poole, and as one of the original members of the RBNA, she complained that it was now 'practically controlled by five medical men ... and their subordinates' and that efforts were being made 'to take all power and even all voice ... out of the hands of the Matrons.'[16] Later in 1897, when it was proposed to admit mental attendants to the RBNA's register of trained nurses by examination, she objected, believing that since they had not undergone three years of rigorous hospital training, 'experience would be replaced by smartness.'[17] During the long campaign for state registration she addressed many public meetings; speaking to the National Union of Women Workers in 1907, she called for 'a minimum standard of knowledge [and] ... legal registration of those [nurses] who conformed to that standard.'[18]

Henrietta Poole was the daughter of a Clerical Fellow and Tutor at Trinity College Dublin. In a short autobiography written in 1895, she reflected on her early life:

> I received a good private education, spending two years of my girlhood abroad with my family in France and Switzerland. I had the advantage of being brought up in a practical manner by a mother who considered her daughters should know how to cook, to make their own dresses, and to manage their money as well as to speak French and German and to know something of music and painting ... [But painting] lacked the human interest, without which I could not work. I never remember a time when I would not readily have given up any amusement for any nursing with which I might be entrusted.[19]

She wrote of her parent's initial opposition to the idea of her becoming a nurse, and 'for seven years my wish to become a nurse had to be put aside.' On her experience of working alongside Gertrude Knight at the Adelaide Hospital, she wrote:

A change in the management of the Adelaide Hospital, Dublin, had resulted in the creation of a Matron and a Superintendent of Nurses ... For four years I had the advantage of her (Miss Knight's) advice and assistance, and, to everyone's surprise, it was proved that it was possible for two women, equally heads of departments, to carry on their work in harmony.

Henrietta Poole died in June 1910. An obituary published in the *British Journal of Nursing* remembered her as 'a most successful trainer of nurses ... [whose] pupils not only revered her as one of the best of Matrons, but loved her as a friend to whom they were indebted for many acts of personal kindness.'[20] As a member of the Matron's Council, she was also remembered as 'a fearless and courageous advocate of its principles.'

As Matron of the Adelaide Hospital, Gertrude Knight was noted for her 'untiring energy and watchful care, as well as her thorough mastery of the many details of her work', which had produced 'the happiest results' for the Hospital. Miss Knight resigned as Matron of the Adelaide in 1892 to take up the post of Matron at the Nottingham General Hospital. While there, she was lauded for her 'gentle, yet none the less effective' talents as Matron of one of England's highest ranked training schools.[21]

Like Miss Poole, Miss Knight was also a member of the RBNA and she too opposed the direction taken by the RBNA after 1892, and was one of the original members of the Matron's Council of Great Britain and Ireland. Later in 1898, she became the Vice-chairman of the Matron's Council. She was also one of the original members of the Society for the State Registration of Trained Nurses, and regularly attended meetings of the Society to campaign for state registration. For civil nursing service as Matron in Nottingham during the Great War, Miss Knight was presented with the Royal Red Cross by King George V in 1917.

The issue of the registration of nurses, which Henrietta Poole and Gertrude Knight so strongly advocated, would come to dominate nursing affairs in Ireland and England for the first two decades of the twentieth century.

Miss Fitzpatrick

Miss Poole's successor as Lady Superintendent was Miss Stewart. Appointed in July 1894 and described as 'a shrewd Scotchwoman', Miss Stewart trained at King's College Hospital in London, was a ward sister at King's, and was later the Night Superintendent at the Royal Free Hospital in Ormond Street. However, Miss Stewart was succeeded soon after in 1896 by Miss J. M.

Fitzpatrick, at which time it appears that the dual management system intro-duced some years earlier was no longer being operated; Miss Fitzpatrick held the title Matron and was, it seems, responsible for the Nursing Department and the Hospital Establishment. Like her predecessors, Miss Fitzpatrick took steps to improve the nursing arrangements where she saw deficiencies. In October 1896, she made the case for hiring additional ward maids, writing:

> It has frequently occurred to me that if the great aim and object of nursing (the skilful and efficient attendance of the sick) is to be realised, some change in the nurses' duties is absolutely necessary. At present a great amount of the nurses' time is taken up in sweeping wards, polishing brass, cleaning baths, kitchens &c. I consider this work might be done much better and in less time by women accus-tomed to it … and patients and nurses would gain immensely … If my suggestion of employing three additional ward maids be approved, and ample accommodation be provided, I feel certain patients would be better cared for and the duties of nurses be performed in a much more satisfactory manner.[22]

The Managing Committee supported her proposal. Like her counterparts in the other Dublin hospitals, Miss Fitzpatrick believed in a thorough and systematic training for nurses. She also held that proper instruction in the theory and practice of sick nursing should include 'a practical knowledge' of sick cookery, and in this connection, she arranged for nurses in training to receive a course of lectures on cookery from a teacher at the Kildare Street School of Cookery in 1902.

Miss Fitzpatrick had a clear understanding of the role of the professionally-trained nurse, and like her predecessors, she was also a prominent matron on the Dublin professional scene. In 1900, she attended the inaugural meeting of the Dublin Nurses' Club, the first professional association of nurses in Ireland, and as a founding member, was elected onto its Committee. The Dublin Nurses' Club was re-constituted in 1904 as the Irish Nurses' Association (INA) and became one of the main professional bodies to cam-paign for state registration of nurses. In 1903, the Society for the State Registration of Trained Nurses was founded in London by Mrs Ethel Bedford Fenwick, and among its members were many prominent Irish matrons of the period, including Margaret Huxley, Annie MacDonnell, Mrs Kildare-Treacy, and Miss Fitzpatrick. In 1904 Miss Fitzpatrick was forced to resign due to ill health, and in appreciation of her services, the Managing Committee pre-sented her with a sum of £50.

The Adelaide probationer

The system of probationership training was described in the hospital's Annual Report for 1889 as follows:

> Every probationer, on first coming to the hospital, must present herself before the Nursing Committee, who decide as to her fitness. If she be accepted, she then binds herself to serve the hospital for three years. During her first year she is trained in the wards as a probationer, and, as far as is practicable, she receives training in each of the four [nursing] divisions. At the end of the first year she is required to present herself for an examination conducted by the Superintendent of Nurses and two members of the medical staff. On passing this examination she becomes eligible to hold the post of staff nurse in one of the wards. At the expiration of the second year she is transferred to the out-nursing department. At the end of the third year, she undergoes a second examination, on passing which she becomes entitled to receive a certificate, and the Nursing Committee then decide whether she shall be placed permanently on the out-nursing staff. In addition to these, ladies wishing to be trained as nurses, by paying a fee for their training, receive the same instruction as other probationers, for one year, but they are not bound to serve the hospital for three years unless they elect so to do.[23]

In common with the other Dublin voluntary hospitals in the period after 1880, the Adelaide recruited young women in their early to mid twenties from the families of merchants, businessmen, farmers, and many Adelaide probationers were also the daughters of clergymen and medical men. Applicants to the Adelaide School were required to be 'of the Protestant faith, fairly well educated (under which head marked attention is expected to the item of reading aloud), not less than 23 years of age and be able to produce to the Board [of Management] a certificate of birth and of good health.'[24]

At this time, the Adelaide operated the 'ordinary' and 'paying' probationer system.[25] This two-class system was common in the late nineteenth century in most of the large voluntary hospitals in England and Ireland. A paying or 'special' probationer was generally recruited from upper middle class families, received no salary and instead paid a substantial fee for training, but was not contractually bound to the hospital when the one-year training period was completed. In 1895, the fee was thirteen guineas a quarter, and having completed just one year of training, a paying probationer who passed the required examinations received a certificate of training and could leave the hospital.

This one-year training period was viewed in the wider nursing world as being 'not at all progressive', and the hospital itself considered that the 'period necessary for full training' was three years, and should a paying probationer opt to remain for full training, she could do so and 'be taught free of charge in return for her service rendered'.[26] With a one-year certificate of training, many paying probationers could earn a good living as private nurses.

Ordinary probationers were in the majority and came from middle class families who were not able to afford the training fees, although they paid a 'nominal fee' of £5.5s for training. They completed three years of training, received a salary, and made up the main body of nurses providing the nursing services in the hospital, as well as in private nursing. The salary paid to probationers in the period was £10 for the first year, £12 for the second and £15 for the third. Some paying probationers became ordinary probationers when family circumstances, such as the death of a father, meant that they could no longer afford the fees.

In the early 1890s, the age of entry was set at twenty-three years, and this rule was strictly applied, even in cases where an applicant was the daughter of gentlemen of high standing or in the case of an applicant when a parent died leaving the family impoverished. All probationers underwent a trial period of three months, and in this period the matron kept 'a record of the personal merits and conduct of each nurse', which she submitted to the Nursing Committee. A further report on each probationer's merits and conduct was submitted to the Nursing Committee at the completion of the three years' training. These reports were not a mere formality but carried considerable importance, particularly for a probationer who was reported to be negligent in her duty. In 1892, for example Miss Poole reported that she had found it her duty to discharge a nurse for acts of disobedience and deceit, which were thoroughly proved and admitted by her.'[27]

Examinations in the theory of sick nursing were conducted by an examination board of three medical men. A special certificate of honour was introduced in 1898 to be awarded, 'as the Examiners may recommend', to a nurse who having passed her final examination had demonstrated 'distinguished answering'.

A day in the life

A probationer's life was built around her work, and the routine of her six-day working week of eighty-seven hours that included off days and half-holidays was punctuated by brief daily rest periods and mealtimes. A course of lectures was given by the Matron and by one or more of the medical officers; Matron and a medical officer each gave one lecture a fortnight, and up to a total of fourteen lectures was given. A description from *The Lady of the House*, published in January 1895, indicates the hours of rest and holidays offered to Adelaide probationers:

> The hours of duty for probationers and trained nurses in [the Adelaide] Hospital is 87 hours per week, and the terms are adjusted so as to come lightly on the workers. The dinner hour may vary. There are two half-holidays in the week, from 3 o'clock to 9 pm; and on Sunday alternately, from 11 am to 2 pm, and from 3 till 9 pm with an additional hour and a half for rest or recreation on four days of the week.

Probationers were expected to attend 'service of prayer read in the Boardroom each Sunday'. Built around work and rest periods, the probationer's day was rigidly structured:

> Nurses going on day duty are called at 6 am, and get tea or coffee, with bread and butter, before they enter the wards; they have breakfast, with meat or eggs, at 8.30; a luncheon of milk and bread and butter in the ward kitchen at 11 o'clock and dinner is served in the dining-hall, presided over by the matron, assistant matron and divisional nurses, from 1.30 to 2.15 pm; five o'clock tea is prepared in the ward kitchens (like the pantry or stillroom of a gentleman's house); and a meat supper is laid in the dining hall at 9 pm. Meals for the night nurses are arranged on a similarly liberal scale, and tea or milk and bread and butter is laid out at 6 each evening for nurses who have been abroad on leave or who have returned from nursing private cases.[28]

The abundance of food in the above description seems rather comforting, but for one former Adelaide nurse, her abiding memory of training was one of always feeling hungry, an experience that she attributed to the very hard physical work that was required for hospital nurse training.[29]

In 1895, probationers attended 'twelve lectures given by the matron, and lectures given by physicians and surgeons, and in the first year of training, probationers completed a two-month period between ... the children's landing, the male landing, the female landing, and Victoria House.'[30] They were also assigned to private out nursing duties during third year. The charge for out nursing in 1892 was £1. 5s per week or 10s and 6d per day, and a charge of 5s was made for massage treatment at each attendance. Each out nurse was expected to return a report on her work, which was completed by either a member of the family that she attended or the family doctor. The report contained the following questions:

1. State the nature of the case nursed
2. Has the nurse been attentive to the patient, good tempered, neat, clean, and careful to carry out the doctor's orders?
3. Have you any faults to find with the nurse, and if so, what are they?

Alice Reeves recalled her arrival at the hospital in 1893 and her introduction to the 'dark airless cubicle' in the Nurses' Home with a bed at least nine inches too short.'[31] She also recalled that when she later returned as a ward sister she had always appreciated the 'great kindness' of the medical staff, and she remembered that Dr James Little's advice to her in dealing with 'recalcitrant probationers' was 'give them a good talking to, Sister, bring tears to their eyes, but never let them overflow.'

In the line of duty

In the late nineteenth century it was common for the major Dublin hospitals to receive requests from other parts of Ireland for the services of their nurses. Conditions for nurses who might be sent on duties to other parts of Ireland could be difficult. In March 1895, the Nursing Committee met to consider the circumstances in which Nurse Hosford had returned from the Sligo Infirmary, having been posted there on the previous day by Miss Stewart to nurse small pox cases.[32] Nurse Hosford gave a detailed account of her experiences while in Sligo. She advised the Committee that on her arrival she was asked by Dr Murray, the Infirmary doctor, to 'oversee the women and to see that the patients get their nourishment'. While her room was 'fairly clean', the smell was 'disagreeable', since it was close to the wards and the lavatories were on either side and she had to eat her meals on a table without a tablecloth. She reported that 'there appeared to be no "Head" to the place' and that the two nurses employed there appeared to be very old, one 80 years and the other 70, and 'none of the women seemed to care to have her in the place.' Her reason for returning to Dublin on the following day was that she 'though it was impossible to get things done'. However, for 'the very serious offence' of leaving the Sligo Infirmary and returning to Dublin without communicating with Miss Stewart and against the wishes of the Infirmary doctor, Nurse Hosford was suspended for three months.

The regime of hard work could take its toll on some probationers, particularly those in 'delicate health' and those attending fever cases. In 1892 one nurse was forced to take leave having been in attendance on four typhoid cases, and the following year two nurses were forced to resign due to ill health. Some nurses paid the ultimate sacrifice in the line of duty; in 1896, Nurse Crookshank died of typhoid fever, 'caught at her first private case'. The daughter of the Reverend C. H. Crookshank, the nurse in question had shown 'extreme devotion to a child having that illness who she was attending', and conveying its sympathy to the nurse's family, the Managing Committee wrote of 'her character and her accomplishments as a nurse'.[33] In June 1899, Nurse Susan MacDonnell also died of typhoid fever, which she contracted while nursing fever cases in Victoria House. In a tribute, Miss Fitzpatrick referred to Nurse MacDonnell's 'gentle, quiet and unobtrusive life'. Her death occurred at a time when there was a lot of sickness among the nurses working in Victoria House, and at that time Miss Fitzpatrick sought its closure for one month for a 'thorough cleaning'.

Risks to health were not the only threat that the probationer faced in this period, and while not common, dismissals from training might be the fate of those probationers who were considered 'not likely to make good nurses' or those who had committed a serious breach of the rules of proper conduct. In 1905, one probationer was asked to resign having entered into inappropriate correspondences with a former patient of the hospital; the probationer's indiscretion involved the exchange of a number of letters written in increasingly 'intimate terms'. In asking the Managing Committee to permit his daughter to return to the hospital, the probationer's father accepted that his daughter was deserving of the 'severest reprimand [for her] one foolish discretion'. Despite the father's plea to 'let mercy have the ascendancy over justice', the Managing Committee upheld the decision to dismiss the probationer.[34]

The Adelaide nurses' uniform

Nurses' uniforms of the period were an outward symbol of the new professional nurse, presenting an image of virtue, hygiene and moral cleanliness, and it distinguished properly trained lady nurses from untrained nurses, and other uniformed women workers, such as ward maids and domestic servants.[35] Two types of uniform were worn, the indoor uniform for ward duty and the outdoor uniform for use when going on and off duty and for travelling in public to nurse private cases. The uniform of the Adelaide Hospital was most distinctive and was described in 1895 as:

> [A] dress of hail spot cotton print, white cap and apron, and small straw bonnet trimmed in blue, with cape-fronted cloak of blue cloth.[36]

The Adelaide dress, with its distinct 'Nightingale spots', was the same as that worn by ward sisters at St Thomas's Hospital, where the Nightingale School was founded in 1860.[37] Strict rules governed the manner of its wearing:

> The uniform ... must be worn at all times within the hospital and out of doors while on nursing work. The wearing of jewellery is prohibited, and an orderly, unostentatious style of dress must be maintained.[38]

A brief controversy concerning the Adelaide nurses' uniform erupted in July 1889, when the Nursing Committee considered a communications from the Red Cross Nursing Institution at Harcourt Street concerning the Adelaide outdoor uniform. The Minutes of the Nursing Committee record the details of the complaint, along with the Committee's response:

> Miss Poole informed the Nursing Committee that she had received two letters, one from the Secretary of the Red Cross Nursing Institution, Harcourt Street, the other from W. Lambert Ormsby, complaining that 'the nursing staff of the Adelaide Hospital had assumed the Outdoor Navy Blue Costume indistinguishable from that which has been worn by the Red Cross Sisters for several years past' and that thereby confusion has arisen. Miss Poole informed the Committee that the uniform of the Adelaide Nurse is alike only in colour, but that in every other way is quite unlike – that the Red Cross Sisters wear a long loose cloak, and have veils to their bonnets, whereas the Adelaide Nurses have tight fitting cloaks, with cape and sleeves, and have no veils to their bonnets, and have white strings. The Nursing Committee recommend that the Secretary write a letter to the Secretary of the Red Cross Nursing Home drawing his attention to the difference and pointing out that as the resemblance between the two uniforms is only one of colour, the Adelaide Nursing Committee fail to see that the Red Cross Nursing Home can claim a monopoly of colour, and that there does not seem any reasonable ground for the complaint of imitation.[39]

While this 'complaint of imitation' on the part of the Red Cross might seem petty, issues of money and snobbery most probably lay at the heart of the complaint. As the Red Cross and Adelaide outdoor nurses went about their private nursing duties on behalf of their respective institutions, failure to distinguish Red Cross and Adelaide nurses might lead to confusion in the public mind. This confusion might, in turn, risk the loss of valued clients to either institution. In addition, the Red Cross Nursing Institution, which was founded by the (Protestant) Dublin Red Cross Nursing Sisters at Harcourt Street in 1884, recruited its lady nurses – described as 'gentlewomen by birth and social position' – exclusively from the upper classes.[40]

The matter was the subject of a news report in *The Nursing Record*, the leading professional journal of the time.[41] Attributed to 'SG', the report seemed to side with the Red Cross position; it mentioned the fact that 'the Dublin Red Cross Nursing Sisterhood recently held a meeting ... [at which] considerable annoyance was expressed that the uniform of the Institution was not only imitated, but actually copied, by other Hospital Sisterhoods, and a formal protest against the practice was ordered to be sent to the Adelaide Hospital.' The reporter commented:

> I have no doubt that the authorities of the latter body will have the courage to give an explanation full and complete, for surely there is sufficient originality and diversity of taste and design in the nursing world to prevent the adoption of other people's ideas. The Adelaide Hospital Nursing Staff no doubt means well by using the style of dress originated by another Institution, but permission might first have been obtained.

The piece was concluded with a more measured request that 'perhaps some of our Dublin friends will enlighten us as to the exact position of affairs in respect to this matter.' The episode did not result in any change of uniform and the Adelaide Hospital hail spot cotton print dress remained the distinguishing feature of the Adelaide nurse for the next century.

The Adelaide abroad

Modern nursing was held in high public regard, and although the work was demanding and the hours long, a position of certified nurse was highly valued among middle class women in the 1890s.[42] In the period there was a waiting list for admission to probationership training at the Adelaide Hospital, and those who held a position of certified nurse rarely resigned, and only did so to marry or pursue a higher position. A few were obliged to resign *in extremis*, such as Nurse Ireland who, following the death of her sister in 1895, was needed at home to help her mother care for three little children. Lilly Elliott resigned in 1889 to 'improve her position' and 'take up [private] nursing on her own account.'[43] Others resigned to take up nursing work abroad in hospitals in Paris, London, and North America.

The Adelaide took great pride in the success of its own nurses and on the occasions when its nurses left to take on new and higher positions, the

Nursing Committee took great pleasure in recording such achievements. The news of Margaret Agnew's appointment as Matron to the Stillorgan Convalescent Home in 1891 when 'there were more than one hundred candidates' was noted with particular pleasure by the Committee. Similarly, reports from employers praising former Adelaide nurses were also recorded with satisfaction, such as that received in 1891 from Dr Playfair of London, who conveyed to the Committee his 'very high praise' for Nurse Sayers.

The Adelaide Hospital nurse could also be found in farer reaches. The campaign for state registration of nurses coincided with the movement for women's suffrage, and many prominent campaigners in the nursing cause were also prominent supporters of the women's cause, including Mrs Ethel Bedford Fenwick, the leading campaigner for nurses' registration. As an example of professional women at work, nursing was featured at the Woman's Building at the World Fair in Chicago in 1893. Among those attending were a number of prominent lady superintendents from Britain and Ireland, including Henrietta Poole. The exhibition contained 'all the newest appliances, such as syringes, thermometers, catheters, douches, inhalers, ice bags, glass and crockery, etc.', and among the exhibits hanging on the walls of the Women's Building were specimens of hospital training certificates that included those of the Adelaide Hospital, as well as St Bart's, Guy's, St George's, and the Royal Infirmary Edinburgh.[44]

Later at an exhibition of nursing appliances in London in 1895, the organisers expressed their delight at the number of Irish matrons, doctors, and laymen who were in attendance, and remarked on 'the evident desire upon the part of those responsible for the care of the sick and training of nurses in Ireland to be up-to-date.' Among those attending was Mr Fry, Treasurer of the Adelaide Hospital, who was described as 'a gentleman far in advance in his views on nursing education of the majority of the gentlemen who are at the heads of our London Nursing Schools [and who] believes in a uniform curriculum of education for nurses, a central examination, and scholarships for nurses.'[45]

CHAPTER FOUR

Celebration and conflict:
The Adelaide School, 1900-1919

Introduction

Christmas 1896 at the Adelaide Hospital was described as 'most enjoyable [with] ... guests being welcomed in most cheery fashion by the Matron, Miss Fitzpatrick, and the Resident Surgeon, Dr Daw.'[1] The visitors to the hospital inspected the wards, which were 'most tastefully decorated [and] an exceptionally attractive concert was held during the afternoon, the audience filling the large hall to its fullest capacity.' At the concert Dr Power O'Donoghue 'kindly conducted, and the music was admirably rendered [and] Mrs Boucher recited a touching piece by Mrs O'Donoghue with grace and earnestness.' The Christmas festivities were an important part of the social life of the Adelaide Hospital, and were also an expression of the essential religious character of the Adelaide.

Three years later in 1899, the Christmas festivities were no doubt marked with added significance as the hospital and the city pondered the dawn of a new century. Modernity had been a strong theme in the late Victorian period, with much public interest in scientific progress, in particular, electricity, transportation, and medical science. The Great Exhibition at the Crystal Palace in 1851 had fired the public imagination about science and set the trend for future scientific exhibitions, such as the World Fair in Chicago in 1892, at which the Adelaide Hospital had a small presence. Many of the great discoveries in scientific medicine had already been made by 1900, including anaesthesia, antiseptics and the germ theory, the significance of which Kendall Franks of the Adelaide was quick to recognise. Large cities had also begun to address the most urgent public health problems of sanitation and waste disposal; by 1863 Dublin had its Vartry reservoir scheme to provide clean water to the city and in 1865 Joseph Bazalgette had given London its extensive underground sewerage system, perhaps the greatest civil engineering feat of the nineteenth century.

The new century would see the theme of modernity continue, and with rapid developments in transport and communications technologies, life in modern cities would change utterly as the new century progressed. There were further advances in scientific medicine, and public optimism about the benefits of science was matched by the myriad of medicinal products and electrical 'treatments' that were available to the health conscious consumer. However, scientific discoveries would also find a ready application, not in health, but in the technology of warfare and would soon contribute to the human calamity that was the Great War.

The new year and the new century also heralded a period of great social change. The death of Queen Victoria in 1901, after sixty-three years on the throne, and the advent of the Edwardian era brought great optimism, a new confidence and a more liberal social outlook. Nowhere was this more evident than among the young socialites of the upper middle classes whose 'darling young things' revelled in the gay social life of summer balls, hunts, and parties.[2] However, the excesses and frivolities of the elite debutante classes only served to illustrate the persistence of the old nineteenth-century problem of the extreme social divide between the classes. The divide was especially evident in Dublin where almost a quarter of the city's population lived in a one-room tenement dwelling, and many of the patients who attended the Dublin hospitals were the victims of these same social conditions.

That other great social divide of the nineteenth-century, the inequality of the sexes, also persisted into the new century, and it was only in 1904 that women were first admitted to Trinity College Dublin, and not until 1918 that the Westminster Parliament finally acted to enfranchise women. The self-confidence and optimism of the new Edwardian era found expression in the women's movement, which was given new impetus in 1903 when Emmeline Pankhurst founded the Women's Social and Political Union. The growing women's suffrage movement, which many nurses actively supported, was also reflected in the growth of women workers' trade unions and in the establishment of professional associations to represent professional women like teachers and nurses. Among the new professional nursing associations that were founded in this period were the Irish Matron's Association (1903), the Irish Nurses' Association (1904) and the College of Nursing (1917). The major professional concern for the new nursing associations in the new century was that of state registration, and senior Adelaide nurses would play their part in what was referred to as the 'nursing question'.

The Adelaide Hospital in 1900

At the turn of the twentieth century, the Adelaide Hospital, which 'by its rules [was] exclusively a hospital for Protestants', had 135 beds, including 32 fever beds, and it also had 24 additional beds in its convalescing home. It had a large outpatient department that treated about 12,000 patients annually of 'all religious denominations, principally Roman Catholics', and it treated medical, surgical, fever, gynaecological and skin diseases, and occasionally, 'under critical circumstances of extreme urgency', admitted Roman Catholics.[3] Protocol required that when a medical officer admitted a Roman Catholic in an emergency he was required to submit a report to the Managing Committee. The old tensions of the nineteenth century concerning the religious character of the Adelaide surfaced from time to time in this period. In 1899, a report published in the *Manchester Courier* charged that 'because the Adelaide Hospital is an exclusively managed Protestant institution the Roman Catholics of Dublin "under no circumstances" allow one of their own creed to be treated there lest they be subjected to proselytising influences'. As on previous occasions, the Managing Committee was obliged to reject the charge by restating its rules and pointing to its record in treating Catholics as outpatients.

The Hospital's peculiar constitutional position rendered it wholly dependent on charitable donations and bequests, and this position was summarised by the hospital authorities in 1901:

> Because the fundamental principle which dedicates the intern benefits to Protestants alone, the hospital is cut off from participation in any Government or Municipal grant, and is entirely dependent for support upon a numerically small body in Ireland.'[4]

Accordingly, the hospital received no Parliamentary or Dublin Corporation grant. At that time its needs were for an enlarged outpatient department, a new operating theatre, and more accommodation for nurses. While debts were a constant for the hospital, it also had an endowment fund, and from time to time received large sums in legacies; for example it received a sum of £5,000 from the will of Mr James Weir, who bequeathed monies to a number of other Dublin hospitals on his death. A ward of the hospital was named in his memory and his portrait was hung in the hospital. Later in 1902, the hospital received an allocation of £3,000 from a bequest made by Lord Iveagh to Dublin hospitals.

With advances in medical science and the need for suitable facilities to treat patients, the hospital was always concerned to ensure that it possessed the most modern facilities for treating patients. The operating theatre at the hospital was a particular cause of concern to the Medical Board in 1899, and the state of the theatre was described in a report prepared by Dr Gordon:

> The roof is so constructed that it is impossible to clean it – the beams

and stanchions afford a lodgement for, on windy days particles of dirt can be seen falling on patients, operator, trays for instruments, &c., on rainy days dirty drops fall in a similar manner. The floor which is made of wood is especially dangerous because the crevices between the boards are constantly saturated with blood and other animal matter, which is liable to putrefaction ... [and] the theatre is very drafty.[5]

Dr Gordon believed that for an operating theatre to 'meet the requirements of modern surgery' it should possess pure air, pure water and good light and have 'some smooth polished impermeable material' for the ceiling, walls and floors, and basins of 'modern construction'. As in all matters associated with achieving improvements in the hospital, money was the main obstacle. In May 1899, the hospital made a public appeal for subscriptions to the estimated cost of £9,000 that was needed to build the new theatre, and also to cover the cost of a much needed new nurses' home and a new dispensary.

Alexandra Nurses' Home

The nurses' accommodation at the time consisted of thirty-one beds in the nurses' home and an additional nine in Victoria House. This was considered insufficient for the existing number of nurses and it also restricted the possibility of employing additional nurses; at the time Miss Fitzpatrick proposed that an additional ten nurses, six for intern nursing and four for out nursing be appointed. Bedrooms were divided into cubicles, which in some instances did not exceed six feet square. A subcommittee was established in 1900 to consider the accommodation for nurses, and having inspected the existing accommodation, reported that it was 'of the opinion that, due attention being given to the health and reasonable comfort of the nurses, the existing space allotted to the forty beds is insufficient for most new nurses'. Since the dining room was the only available room for recreating and study, the subcommittee proposed an additional twelve beds along with a new sitting room and a 'smaller room where nurses preparing for an examination could study'. The plans for the new nurses' home were drawn up, and appealing for public donations to build the home, the Managing Committee made a special case for support:

> Surely no one who has known the unspeakable comfort and solace of an adequately taught nurse in the time of sore bodily distress could grudge some little help, that during her long period of training she may experience something of the comforts of home.[6]

The special appeal netted almost £600. The provision of comfortable accommodation for nurses in training meant good conditions of employment and the possibility of attracting the 'better class' of nurse so desired by the reformers of some two decades previously. The supervision of nurses while off duty was also an integral part of the training regime for nurses at the time, and in anticipation of the opening of the new home, a Superintendent of the Nurses' Home (Home Sister) was appointed in May 1902. The new Home Sister was Margaret Vaggis, and advising her of the duties associated the role of Home Sister, the Honorary Secretary of the Managing Committee Mr T. Pakenham Law wrote:

> [Your duties] will include the care and oversight of all the resident nurses and out nurses when in the Home. The [Managing] Committee want the nurses to be mothered and to feel that there is someone to care specially for them; to see after them if unwell, to see that nurses going out and coming in are provided for in food and everything necessary.[7]

The new nurses' home and the new operating theatre were officially opened by Lord Dudley, the Lord Lieutenant, on 15 December 1902, and the home was named the Alexandra Nurses' Home in honour of Queen Alexandra, wife of the new King. At the ceremony Lord Dudley remarked that 'the opening of the new operating theatre brought very forcibly to his mind the anxiety through which he had recently been passing', since his wife, the Lady Dudley, had recently been a patient at the hospital, and he thanked the Adelaide surgeons who had so skilfully attended her.[8]

At the time when the Adelaide was building its new nurses' home and operating theatre, the new biscuit factory of W&R Jacob was under construction just across the street, and during the summer of 1899 this caused a considerable nuisance for the hospital. With the noise of work taking place throughout the night, staff were unable to sleep, and Miss Fitzpatrick was compelled to write to the Managing Committee on a number of occasions about the nuisance. In June 1900, she complained that 'the continual buzzing and vibrating of the machinery ...[was] most wearying to the brain and certainly telling to the health of some of us', and she reminded the Managing Committee that nurses' health was 'our stock-in-trade and we cannot afford to trifle with it.'[9] While wearying, the noise of building work was quite innocent when compared to the noises that would later emanate from the same building when republican volunteers occupied the factory in the Easter Rebellion of 1916.

In 1900, some important changes in the training of nurses were instituted. These included the rule that nurses 'be bound to serve four years instead of three'. The introduction of a training fee of £15 for all nurses was also approved. The only circumstances in which a trainee would be admitted for less than four years were for women embarking on missionary work. The rules for the admission of probationers stipulated that a successful applicant should 'wait her turn'. While this rule was strictly followed, exceptions were made from time to time, such as when Lady Dudley petitioned the Managing Committee to grant early admission to one applicant.

Reports

Evidence from Matron's reports from this period indicates that much emphasis was placed on the nurse's character, intelligence, capabilities as a nurse, and her health.[10] Terms and expressions used to describe good practical nurses included 'satisfactory in every way', 'very capable and dependable', 'very kind to her patients', and 'much liked by patients', and common adjectives used were 'painstaking', 'careful', 'capable', and 'trustworthy'. Some nurses were reported as being 'bright and intelligent', while the intelligence of others was questioned; one nurse was described in a series of reports as 'not very bright but anxious to learn', 'not brilliant', and 'headless at times'. Another was described as 'satisfactory and industrious [but] not clever.' At the end of her first year in 1906, one nurse was described as 'a most promising probationer – quite above the ordinary', and by the end of her training she was considered to be 'a bright intelligent and capable nurse'. Matron's reports on nurses who were not performing well included commentaries such as 'requires looking after', 'careless and irresponsible', and 'conduct not favourable'. An unfavourable report described one nurse as 'a lazy incompetent woman, much disliked by the patients'. Another was reported to be 'a good nurse, but manner not good in the wards, and not a favourite with the patients'. One nurse who completed her training in 1905 was described as 'good at her work, but not a good influence with the other nurses [being] most difficult and dictatorial to work with.'

A nurse's appearance was also frequently commented on by Matron; a nurse could be 'tidy', 'neat' or 'untidy'. A nurse's health was also the subject of Matron's attention, and common adjectives used were 'good' or 'delicate', and a number of nurses 'not strong enough to continue' were forced to end their training prematurely in this period due to ill health. The evidence indicates that rotation to Victoria House was often a precursor to sickness and enforced retirement from training. For example, in 1909, a nurse was 'warded with Scarlet Fever' while working in Victoria House and was later forced to resign. One nurse was reported to have a 'tendency to anaemia', another had a 'tendency to rheumatism', and many were treated for septic finger.

Royal visit

The naming of the new nurses' home in honour of the King's consort Queen Alexandra was just one of many connections between the hospital and the Royal Family, a connection which began with the naming of the hospital in 1838, and continued with the naming of the Victoria Wing to commemorate Queen Victoria's golden jubilee in 1887.

On the afternoon of 14 April 1900, Princess Christian, third daughter of Queen Victoria, visited the Adelaide Hospital and was taken on a tour of inspection of the hospital wards. The Princess was a member of the Royal entourage that was visiting Ireland on the occasion of the Royal visit of the Queen, then in her eighty-first year. The Princess was received at the main entrance by Lord Iveagh and by other members of the Hospital Managing Committee, and was presented with a bouquet of flowers by Mrs Ormsby, wife of the Chairman of the Trustees. Also present were the members of the medical staff, and Miss Fitzpatrick and her assistant Miss Craig greeted the royal visitor and accompanied her on her tour of inspection.[11]

After the visit of Princess Christian, Queen Victoria 'spontaneously announced that she proposed to visit the hospital', and on 17 April, accompanied by the Princess, visited the Adelaide. The visit was one of several Royal visits to Dublin hospitals during her three-week visit to Ireland, and she also visited the nearby Meath Hospital on the same day. Her Landau carriage travelled from the vice regal lodge in the Phoenix Park via Rialto and the South Circular Road and was escorted by the 2nd Life Guards and with equerries riding.[12] The members of the Managing Committee and Miss Fitzpatrick were presented to Her Majesty, and addressing Miss Fitzpatrick, the Queen remarked: 'I am told you have a beautiful hospital here.' The minutes of the Managing Committee record that 'her Majesty was well received by the crowds which filled Peter Street from end to end.' In her journal, the Queen later recorded her recollection of the visit:

> We drove ... to the Adelaide Hospital, situated in the very poorest part of town. The street in which it stands is a very narrow one and the people literally thronged round the carriage, giving me the most enthusiastic welcome, as indeed I received anywhere. Lord Denbeigh awaited me at the hospital and presented the Committee of

Management, as well as the doctors and Lady Superintendent, Miss Fitzpatrick, who gave me a bouquet.[13]

Some days following the Queen's visit to the hospital and while she was still in Ireland, Princess Christian sent to the hospital for a nurse to attend to the Queen's courier who was suffering from pneumonia, and on the following day 'by Her Majesty's own commands a second nurse was sent to aid in the attendance.' In the following June, Her Majesty presented a print portrait of herself to the hospital 'in recollection of her recent visit'.

During the Royal visit, Miss Fitzpatrick was among a large group of more than thirty Dublin matrons who were presented to the Queen at the Viceregal Lodge in the Phoenix Park to welcome Her Majesty to Ireland and to thank her for her interest in nursing. A contemporary report of the visit records details of the meeting with the Matrons:

> The Matrons of the Dublin Hospitals assembled on the afternoon of Thursday at the Viceregal Lodge to the number of thirty-three ... The Matrons formed into line in front of the Viceregal Lodge, and as the Queen drove out the carriage approached the Matrons, and Her Majesty signified her pleasure that the senior Matron, Miss Huxley, should be presented. The presentation having been made, and Her Majesty having graciously conversed with Miss Huxley for a few moments, the Queen passed slowly along the line, bowing and smiling charmingly to all in turn. Her Majesty shortly afterwards retired, and the Matrons were then entertained to tea in the Lodge. The company were also photographed in the grounds, and left the Viceregal Lodge shortly after five o'clock, charmed and pleased with their experience.[14]

Margaret Huxley, the Matron of Sir Patrick Dun's Hospital, on whose suggestion the meeting took place, gave the address on behalf of the matrons and nurses of Dublin:

> May it please Your Majesty, We ... offer our heartfelt greetings on the occasion of your visit to Dublin. We beg to tender our gratitude for the gracious interest which Your Majesty and the Royal Family have shown in fostering the progress of trained nursing of the sick from the time of its initiation by Miss Florence Nightingale. We also desire to express the great happiness we feel at your presence amongst us, and we earnestly trust that your sojourn in Ireland may be of much benefit to Your Majesty's health.[15]

The royal visit to Ireland in 1900 was a joyous experience for the elderly Queen and her daughter and consort Princess Christian. However, the joy of Princess Christian would be short lived, as she was to lose her son in the Boer War later in the same year, and her mother the Queen died in the following year. On learning of the death of the Queen, the Hospital Managing Committee sent a telegram of sympathy to the new King Edward VII, in which they mentioned their privilege at being 'favoured with a special visit from Her Majesty' in 1900, and pledged their loyalty to the Throne. Later on a visit to Ireland in 1903, the new King and Queen were again assured of the loyalty of the Managing Committee, and in reply, the King thanked the ladies and gentlemen for their 'hearty greetings' and assurances of loyalty on the occasion of the visit, and he rejoiced 'to hear of a newly-awakened spirit of hope and enterprise among my Irish people, which is full of promise for the future'.

Soon after the Royal visit, Miss Craig, Assistant Matron was appointed to succeed Miss Fitzpatrick in 1904, and Agnes Lawlor, then the most senior divisional nurse, was appointed Assistant Matron. Miss Craig was, in turn, succeeded by Miss Pate in 1907. Like Miss Fitzpatrick, both Miss Craig and Miss Pate were active in professional affairs and, as members of the Irish Matron's Association, they attended meetings in the city to discuss the pressing concerns of the day, including the question of state registration for nurses. Miss Pate was among a large delegation of Irish matrons who attended the International Congress of Nurses hosted by the ICN in London in July 1909. At the Congress many papers were read on the subject of private nursing, nurse training, and state regulation of nursing.

The happy scenes associated with the Royal visit of 1900 seemed to set the tone for the new century, and while the death of the Queen soon after her visit to Dublin was marked with mourning, her long and great life was celebrated, and the accession of Edward to the throne was also celebrated in Ireland and throughout the kingdom. The optimism of the new modern era included the hope among supporters of Irish home rule that their campaign, which had been ongoing since the 1880s, would soon achieve its goals. However, the Edwardian period was over in less than a decade with the death of King Edward VII in 1910. Home rule was not yet achieved, extreme poverty persisted in the tenements around Peter Street and elsewhere in Dublin city, and darker clouds of conflict, both at home and abroad, would soon appear on the horizon to replace the optimism of the Edwardian period.

The Great War

For Ireland the Great War was not some conflict in a far distant land, but was a war that was being waged against the Kingdom of Great Britain and Ireland, and its impact in Ireland was felt in a number of ways. More than 35,000 Irish soldiers died in the Great War – over 50,000 when those enlisted in the English and Scottish regiments are included – and many more were invalided and suffered lifelong disabilities. Many of the injured soldiers were treated in Ireland in military and civilian hospitals and many nurses and doctors volunteered for military service in Europe and at the home front. In Ireland the principal military hospitals were at Cork (88 beds), the Curragh in County Kildare (302 beds), the King George V Military Hospital at Arbour Hill in Dublin (462 beds), and the Ulster Volunteer Force Hospital at Craigavon in County Armagh.[16] In addition, a number of civilian hospitals were partly commissioned as military hospitals – these included the Royal City of Dublin Hospital and the Adelaide Hospital – and some private individuals, including Harold Pim of Monkstown House, donated buildings for use as auxiliary hospitals.[17] In the military hospitals, wounded soldiers were treated by the Royal Army Medical Corps (RAMC) and the nursing care was provided by the Queen Alexandra's Imperial Military Nursing Service (QAIMNS). From 1914 until early 1917, up to 12,000 wounded soldiers were removed to Ireland on hospital ships and distributed to the various military and civilian hospitals around the country.[18] In the later years of the war, as the threat of German U-boats emerged – the *Lusitania* with almost 1,200 men, women and children was lost off the Old Head of Kinsale – fewer wounded soldiers were transported by ship to Dublin, and this greatly eased the burden on the military and civilian hospitals.[19]

The Adelaide Hospital played its part in the Great War, particularly in the first three years of the war, the period in which hospital ships operated before the threat of German U-boats. Victoria House was the hospital's fever wing containing thirty-eight beds, and along with an additional twelve beds, it was commissioned as an exclusively military hospital where many hundreds of soldiers were treated for wounds and related illnesses. Containing twenty four beds, the Featherstonhaugh Convalescent Home in Rathfarnham was also commissioned as a military hospital during the War. While the hospital was an independent institution, the War Office had the power to inspect it or any other civilian hospital in which beds were requisitioned for military use.

All of the Hospital's surgical staff in the period served with the army or Red Cross in France, including Mr Gunn, Mr Pearson, and Dr Harvey.

Louisa Bewley, who for many years was a member of the Adelaide Board, worked as a VAD during the War. Adelaide nurses also gave service as members of the Queen Alexandra's Royal Army Nursing Corps. By the end of 1917, a total of eight sisters and twenty-seven nurses had given active service. Among the nurses to go on active service at the start of the war were Annie McIntosh (Co Dublin), Annie Mills (Co Armagh), Ethel O'Neill (Co Wexford), Florence Forde (Co Down), Isobel Tyndall (Co Dublin), Isabella Gawley (Co Sligo), Rita Arnold (Co Down), Margaret Boland (Co Mayo), and Beatrice Bryan (Dublin). Others to go on active service after 1915 included Jessie Allan Jones (Co Carlow), Alice MacDonald (Dublin City), Grace E. Stewart (Limerick), Ethel Elizabeth Haskins (Co Tipperary), Daisy Elizabeth Pratt (Co Cavan), Martha Lundy (Co Armagh), Georgina Hester Salter (Co Cork), Frances Adele Hayward (Co Dublin), Minnie Moody (Co Derry), Gladys Johnson (Co Wicklow), Dora Harvey (Dublin), Muriel Treanor (Co Dublin), and Helen Fitzgerald (Co Laois).[20] A number on the home front were honoured for their services. Miss Lawlor, the Matron of the Fetherstonhaugh Convalescent Home, received the Second Class Red Cross Decoration in person from King George VI, for her services to the care of wounded soldiers during the war. Miss P. H. Hill, who was Matron and Superintendent of Nursing during the war years held the title RRC (Royal Red Cross). As many as twelve individuals associated with the Adelaide made the ultimate sacrifice in the Great War, among them nurse E. G. Stewart.[21]

The nurses' register for the early years of the war indicates that a number failed to complete training, either leaving or simply not returning from leave. With no explanation recorded, it may be that some were the daughters or sisters of family members lost in the war.

Aside from the added burden of treating the war wounded, the war brought other problems for the hospital, most especially financial. While the government in London paid the hospital a grant for the treatment and care of wounded soldiers, as with all wars, great economic hardship attended the conflict. The cost of most goods, especially food, fuel, drugs and surgical appliances, had almost doubled in price in the years since the commencement of the war. The financial burden was so great that ward closures were considered and a special appeal for donations was made. One response was the establishment of the 'Matron's 100,000 Half-Crown Fund'. Through the Fund, Miss Hill succeeded in raising sufficient monies to ease the financial difficulties in 1919, and in the following year the Fund realised a sum of over £9,000. In that same year the monies contributed by the Dublin Hospital Sunday Fund amounted to £854. Income was also augmented by donations, subscriptions and legacies and by monies received from the government for the care of army and navy Pensioners. At that time the hospital also earned considerable additional income from monies which patients gave as a contribution to the cost of their hospital treatment.

By the end of 1920 the financial state of the hospital had greatly improved, and the total number of nurses employed was sixty six, of whom ten were sisters, and fifty six were nurses and probationers. The hospital also provided training for a small number of Red Cross probationers in the period. Even after the war had ended, the hospital continued to treat soldiers who had returned from the military campaign overseas. War veterans were treated for a variety of problems, including malaria, dysentery, 'rheumatism contracted in the trenches', various other diseases, and shell shock. Many who were victims of gas poisoning were treated for bronchitis for many years after the war ended. In 1922 the War Pensions Committee sent 361 sick pensioners to the Adelaide for treatment, but by 1925 this number had gradually declined to just 92.

In 1918, when the war in Europe was claiming several million young lives, even the killing efficiency of the howitzers and machine guns could not match the efficiency of a new killer, the influenza virus, which, like the guns, had a propensity for killing young adults. The influenza pandemic of 1918-1919 would claim many more lives than the Great War, and Ireland was not spared; upwards on a million Irish people were infected and it is estimated that twenty thousand died in the pandemic in Ireland. The Adelaide Hospital experienced firsthand the effects of the pandemic. In 1918 with the added work of treating flu victims for associated pneumonia, a large number of the nursing staff succumbed to influenza, throwing 'a very great strain' on those members of the nursing staff that were able to remain on duty. The situation was helped somewhat at the time by the assistance given by Voluntary Aid Detachment (VAD) nurses. Former Adelaide medical student Kathleen Lynn was prominent in providing medical relief for children in Dublin who were the victims of the epidemic, and she established a small children's hospital in a house that she purchased in Charlemont Street.[22]

1916 Rising

While Ireland's fields and streets were spared the horrors of the military conflict in Europe, the guns of battle were to echo across Dublin when many parts of the city saw fierce fighting in the republican uprising of Easter 1916. Led by the Irish Republican Brotherhood and the Irish Citizen's Army, the week-long conflict was fought out in many of the city's public buildings. The guns of battle sounded around the Adelaide Hospital when groups of republican volunteers, attacking the Ship Street Barracks beside Dublin Castle and the Portobello Barracks to the south, occupied the biscuit factory of W&R Jacob Ltd, across the street from the hospital. They also occupied the nearby Royal College of Surgeons and other local buildings on Aungier Street and Wexford Street.[23] Thomas MacDonagh commanded the rebels, who numbered up to 150 volunteers, including a small number of women volunteers attached to Cumann na mBan.[24]

The Adelaide Hospital treated as many as seventy wounded and received some dead from the conflict taking place on its doorstep, and for a short time during the fighting the hospital was cut off from its food supplies. The hospital was directly overlooked by the Jacob's factory, and rebels occupying the upper floors at the Peter's Row side of the factory came under machine gunfire from the tower at Dublin Castle.[25] William James Stapleton, one of the volunteers occupying the Jacob's factory, gave an eyewitness account of the death of one of the volunteers:

> Immediately on entering Stephen's Green West, fire was opened on us, I think, from the top of Grafton St, and one of our volunteers was wounded turning into York Street. We succeeded in getting him back to Jacob's factory where he received treatment and was removed subsequently to the Adelaide Hospital where I understand he was operated on, but he died. I think this man's name was McGrath. I went back to my post and remained there until Sunday morning. When we brought the wounded McGrath into the building there was considerable distress evident among the small party of girls present from Cumann na mBan who were in charge of cooking and attached to the First Aid station.[26]

For a brief period on Easter Tuesday, the Adelaide Hospital risked attack by the rebels, when a rumour spread among them that all the patients were being moved to the rear of the hospital to make ready the front for occupation by the military.[27] However, the attack did not happen. While many buildings occupied by the rebels were shelled by the British forces, the Jacob's factory was spared from such an attack; in Mitchell's view the factory's proximity to the Adelaide Hospital, and the fact that the hospital was an institution owned and run by Protestant unionists explains the British decision in the circumstances.[28] The volunteers at the Jacob's factory were the last to surrender in the uprising, and the leaders of those who occupied the factory, including Commandant MacDonagh, John MacBride and Michael O'Hanrahan, were among those executed for treason in the aftermath of the rebellion.

An old battle: State registration

The battles on the streets of Dublin and in the trenches of Europe resulted in many horrific injuries, and the new technology of warfare presented surgeons and nurses with new challenges in treating wounds never before witnessed.[29] Added to this were the challenges of treating the long-term effects of chemical weapons on the respiratory system and the psychological trauma of shell shock. New techniques in surgery, wound care and rehabilitation were being developed, and nurses' professional training needed to be responsive to these developments. While skilled nursing demanded thorough and systematic training, the situation remained that any woman could use the title 'nurse' and could advertise her services for private nursing. Nursing leaders believed that the public good and the good of nursing were not well served as long as this situation continued. While the introduction of proper training had reformed nursing and the hospitals, for the nursing leaders who came after Nightingale, the reform of nursing could not be complete until nursing became regulated by the state, and become a *de jure* profession.

The regulation of nursing by the state, today so much taken for granted by nurses and the general public, was hard won and achieved only after a long and often bitter campaign that lasted for nearly thirty years. In the long running campaign, divisions among senior nurses and other vested interests were a constant feature. In the early years of the campaign Florence Nightingale opposed nurses' registration, believing that the personal and moral qualities needed to be a nurse could not be tested in a state examination.[30] Nightingale's emphasis on vocational commitment was rejected by the pro-registrationists, led by Mrs Ethel Bedford Fenwick, who called for complete state regulation involving a standardised curriculum and a professional register of nurses. Irish nurses campaigned for state regulation through the Irish Matron's Association (IMA) and the Irish Nurses' Association (INA), and Margaret Huxley and former Adelaide nurse Alice Reeves were the leading campaigners in Ireland. In evidence to a Select Committee of the House of Commons, established in 1904 to examine the 'nursing question', Huxley called for the establishment of a 'central authority' to regulate nursing, so that 'the public would be assured that they (nurses) know their work … and that they must be reputable women at least because their hospitals must have vouched for them and kept them for three year's work.'[31] The medical profession generally supported state regulation, but some medical men who were members of hospital managing committees opposed it.

In January 1904, the Managing Committee of the Adelaide Hospital received a correspondence from Mrs Bedford Fenwick, seeking support for a nurses' registration bill sponsored by the Society for the State Registration of Nurses, of which Miss Fitzpatrick was then a member.[32] While the Bill was not supported by parliament, it placed the nursing question on the agenda of parliamentarians and created a wider public awareness of the subject. After 1904, a series of nurses' registration bills failed to get parliamentary approval, due in part to the lack of unity among nurses, and also due to opposition from powerful voluntary hospitals that feared control by the state in their affairs. These included Guy's and the London Hospital, whose influential Matron, Eva Luckës, believed in the superiority of nurse training at the elite voluntary hospitals.[33] There is no evidence of any concerted campaign against registration in the Dublin hospitals, and the matrons of all the major Dublin hospitals, including Miss Hill, were active members of the Irish Matron's Association, which supported state registration.

Disunion

In 1916, the College of Nursing was founded in London to promote the advancement of nursing as a profession, and in March 1917, an Irish Board of the College of Nursing was established, with a membership of twenty-two that included twelve senior nurses, representatives of the medical profession, and lay people. Its members included Miss Egan, President of the Irish Matron's Association, Miss Eddison, Royal City of Dublin Hospital, and Miss Hill, the Adelaide Hospital.[34] In a move to oppose the College of Nursing and its scheme for a voluntary register of trained nurses, Margaret Huxley and other senior matrons not affiliated with the College of Nursing in Ireland, including Miss Reeves, Dr Steevens' Hospital, and Miss Bradbourne, Meath Hospital, founded the Irish Nursing Board. The new Irish Nursing Board was heralded as a very democratic body which, unlike the College of Nursing, would be 'almost entirely in the hands of nurses'.[35]

In 1918, legislation proposing the registration of nurses was before parliament, and two bills were under consideration, one sponsored by the Royal British Nurses' Association (RBNA) and the other by the College of Nursing. At the time there were rumours that the College of Nursing would in future conduct all final examinations for nurses and would have disciplinary powers over them. Such rumours were reported to be causing 'considerable apprehension' among nurses, and many of the major training hospitals whose matrons supported the College of Nursing bill were obliged to issue public statements on the matter. In a letter published on 21 September 1918 in the *British Journal of Nursing*, Miss Hill clarified the position of the Nursing

Committee of the Adelaide Hospital, which indicated its intention to act only on the basis of whatever legislation was put in place:

> I am directed by the Nursing Committee to inform you that should the Nurses' Registration Bill, drafted by the College of Nursing Ltd., become law, the probationers at this hospital will enter for examinations conducted by the Statutory Authority set up by that Bill. In the event of the Bill not passing into law, the nurses of this hospital will have the option of entering for the examinations of the College of Nursing Ltd. The Board of Governors will retain the final qualifying examination of the hospital as at present conducted until such time as they deem it advisable in the interest of the nurses and the public that such examinations should be abrogated.[36]

The Royal City of Dublin Hospital also published a letter in the *BJN* stating that the rumours were 'unfounded and inaccurate.' Lieutenant-Colonel Dean of the Royal Victoria Hospital Belfast was a little more circumspect, stating that the matter had 'not been considered by my Committee, and as I do not know whether the report you have heard is correct or not, I am sorry I cannot give you any information about it.'[37]

In the event, neither of the two registration bills was successful, and instead, a government-sponsored nurses' registration bill, promoted by Dr Addison, the Minister for Health, became law in 1919, finally establishing state regulation of nursing. In the same year a separate Nurses Registration (Ireland) Act was passed into law, creating the General Nursing Council for Ireland, the first state regulatory body for nursing in Ireland. While the new legislation reflected the position taken by the pro-registrationists led by Margaret Huxley, Alice Reeves and the Irish Nursing Board, the new General Nursing Council was made up of representatives from both the Irish Nursing Board and the Irish Board of the College of Nursing, as well as representatives of the Irish Matron's Association.[38]

Alice Reeves
Alice Reeves, the daughter of a clergyman and granddaughter of the Bishop of Down, entered training at the Adelaide in 1893. She became a divisional nurse in 1900 and after fifteen years at the Adelaide was appointed Matron of the Royal Victoria Eye and Ear Hospital in 1908, and in 1918 she became Matron of Dr Steevens' Hospital.[39] She was a founding member of the Irish Nurses Association and the Irish Matrons Association, and served as president of both associations. She was one of the leading campaigners for state

registration, and with Margaret Huxley, founded the Irish Nursing Board and lobbied parliamentarians at Westminster on the nursing question. For many years she was a member of the General Nursing Council of Ireland and sat on important committees of the Council. Alice Reeves was a founding member and the first President of the Adelaide Nurses' League. She resigned as Matron of Dr Steevens' Hospital owing to ill health in 1948 and died in 1950.

Celebration

The disunion among senior nurses in Ireland in the final years of the campaign for nursing regulation did not appear to result in any lasting animosity, and at a dinner hosted by Margaret Huxley at the Bonne Bouche Restaurant in Dawson Street in January 1920 to celebrate the passing of the new registration Act, all the senior matrons were in attendance, including Miss Hill, Miss Phelan, and Miss McGivney, who were members of the Irish Board of the College of Nursing. A report of the celebratory dinner was carried in the *BJN*:

> The dining-room was charmingly arranged with oval mahogany tables artistically set out with shining glass and silver and decorated with mimosa and violets, the blue frocks of the waitresses striking an effective note against buff coloured walls. The dinner of seven courses made one feel that the past five years were as a dream, and that the Lamp of Aladdin must have been used to conjure back days of plenty and delight when pleasant faces and pretty frocks were an ordinary sight. Miss Huxley occupied the chair, on her right hand Miss Michie, President of the Irish Matrons' Association, on her left Miss Reeves, President of the Irish Nurses' Association. The health of His Majesty the King having been proposed and duly honoured, Miss Huxley welcomed her guests.[40]

Miss Huxley gave a speech thanking the members of the Irish Matron's Association for their efforts and saying that 'we may congratulate ourselves that our determination in the past was a strong factor in the framing of this broadly-conceived Act.'[41] In her speech she made special mention of her friend and 'courageous, valiant, and indomitable leader' Mrs Bedford Fenwick, who led the campaign for state registration. Not one to rest on her long-awaited success of achieving state regulation and always progressive in her thinking, Huxley called on the Irish Matrons Association 'to work altogether for the common good, not one training school against another, and this I think could most effectively be done by co-operation [through] a central school.'[42]

Not since the visit of Queen Victoria in 1900 had there been such a large and distinguished gathering of Dublin matrons, coming together in a mood of celebration and optimism. Margaret Huxley had been present in 1900, leading the matrons of Dublin and promoting the nursing cause in the presence of Queen Victoria, and here she was twenty years later, again at the head of the Dublin matrons, but with her major goal achieved. As Miss Hill and the other Dublin matrons celebrated the passing of the new legislation, they must have reflected on the long journey that had ended on that January evening in Dawson Street. It is likely that Miss Hill also pondered the future and what the new situation of state regulation would mean for nurse training at the Adelaide Hospital.

CHAPTER FIVE

'A certain distinction':
The Adelaide School, 1921-1949

With the passing of the Nurses Registration (Ireland) Act in 1919, nursing was now a fully regulated profession and only those nurses trained in an approved training hospital could hold the title 'nurse'. This was a great step forward for nursing and the wider public. In January 1920, as Miss Hill and the other nursing leaders in Dublin celebrated their great achievement in gaining state registration, the country was in the throes of political and military conflict. With the British Government's response to the 1916 uprising, which included executions of the leaders of the uprising, public support for the republican cause resulted in a Sinn Féin victory in the 1918 General Election. This was followed by a declaration of independence and the assembly of the first Irish parliament in 1919. The Anglo-Irish War of Independence that followed was ended with the Anglo-Irish Treaty of December 1921 and the establishment of the new Free State Government. However, conflict continued for another two years when a bitter civil war was waged by supporters and opponents of the Treaty.

When the Civil War ended in 1923, there followed a period of relative peace for the new Irish Free State and the new and separate Northern Ireland State. Great economic hardships, in part the result of the 'economic war' with Britain, marked this period, and like the other voluntary hospitals, the Adelaide experienced the effects of these hardships, with the ever present threat of ward closures.

In this period, the Adelaide was one of twenty-five hospitals in Dublin, and with growing demands on hospital services, principally the result of advances in medical technology in areas like radiology and surgery, financial problems were ever present.[1] These problems were compounded by declines in charitable funding and in the value of endowments. Through the Hospitals Commission, the Free State government contributed to the funding of the voluntary hospitals, and as the hospitals grew to depend more on state grants, and later, on Hospital Sweepstake funds, their independence was threatened.[2] However, the hospitals always fought to maintain their independence and none more so than the Adelaide Hospital, whose constitution forbade it from taking state assistance.[3] While the Sweepstakes scheme, introduced in 1929, gave a great injection of money into the hospitals, the Adelaide viewed the scheme as 'objectionable to the supporters of ... [an essentially] religious institution.' The non-participation of the hospital in the Sweepstake scheme placed it in a difficult financial position throughout the middle decades of the twentieth century, and fundraising and charitable donations continued to be its major source of income.

The Adelaide thus remained as one of the most independent of the voluntary hospitals in this period. Nevertheless, the regulation of nurse training represented a form of state control, albeit a benign one and one that ultimately benefitted the quality of care. In 1920, the Adelaide was granted a Royal Charter, effectively reconstituting the hospital as the Adelaide Hospital Dublin, and after 1922 the Hospital Managing Committee became the Board of Management.

Special appeals for subscriptions and bequests, like the Matron's Annual Pound Day Appeal, and the Dublin Hospital Sunday Fund annual grant remained important sources of income. Aside from the approximate 130 salaried staff, the hospital also relied on the good will of volunteer staff who contributed to the daily work of the various clinical departments, including the laboratories. At the time, the total number of beds was 169, and it was customary to close hospital beds each summer for cleaning and staff holidays. In the early 1930s, the hospital was treating in excess of 2,000 inpatients and over 47,000 outpatients. Over a thousand patients were anaesthetised each year, and the development of better anaesthetic equipment as well as the employment of anesthetists led to a situation where no anaesthesia-related deaths were recorded for many years. In 1928, the Victoria House was reconstructed, and plans for the construction of a private wing and additional accommodation for nurses were announced by the Adelaide Board in 1936.

Regulation and affiliation

After 1920, state regulation was the responsibility of the new General Nursing Council for Ireland, which was empowered to keep a Register of Nurses, prescribe the duration of training and the required experience in sick nursing, and regulate the conduct of state examinations.[4] Entry to the Register was conditional on a nurse successfully completing the prescribed training and passing the state examinations. The Council Rules specified minimum standards for training, including the minimum number of patients required in a training hospital, minimum hours of classroom and ward instruction, and 'adequate staff and equipment for teaching.'[5] The Rules prescribed the duration of training as 'at least three years' in medical and surgical nursing, and prescribed instruction in anatomy, physiology, hygiene, bacteriology, *materia medica*, medical and surgical nursing, fever nursing, nursing ethics, and invalid cookery.[6] With the advent of state regulation, training hospitals were required to apply to the General Nursing Council for approval as a training school.[7] The Adelaide was among the first of eleven Dublin hospitals to gain approval in 1923.[8]

Similar to other training hospitals, the Adelaide's course of lectures was planned around the nurse's work and rest schedule, involving attendance at a morning or evening lecture, and also attendance at a Sunday lecture.[9] At the time lectures were given by the hospital physicians and surgeons, by the Sister Tutor, Miss Taylor, and by Miss Hill. Miss Taylor resigned in 1921 and in 1925, after fourteen years of 'splendid service', Miss Hill retired in order to marry. Miss Hill was remembered as a 'tall striking woman, with ivory complexion ... severe and charming.'[10] Her successor was Miss S. K. Stewart, formerly the Assistant Matron at the Royal Victoria Hospital, Belfast. In that year the complement of nurses was ten sisters and forty-seven nurses and probationers, including out-nurses.

Dublin Metropolitan Technical School for Nurses

Following the introduction of state examinations, many hospitals introduced a period of protected classroom and ward instruction in the first months of training. This period was termed the 'preliminary training school' since it was aimed at preparing probationers for the General Nursing Council's Preliminary Examination.[11] In 1937, the preliminary training period at the Adelaide School was six weeks of classroom instruction followed by two four-week periods of ward instruction.

After state registration, the Adelaide Hospital became affiliated with the Dublin Metropolitan Technical School for Nurses, as a way of providing a more regular system of lectures. The school was founded in 1893 by Margaret Huxley to provide 'a place for the better technical education of nurses in Dublin', and is reputed to be the first centralised nurse training school in the world.[12] Before 1920, five institutions, including Dr Steevens' and Sir Patrick Dun's hospitals, were affiliated with the school. After the establishment of the General Nursing Council, the school took on a greater prominence in nurse training in Dublin, when many more of the Dublin hospitals became affiliates. The Adelaide was one of the first to affiliate in 1922, and many others followed, including the Meath, Mercer's, the Royal City of Dublin, and the Children's Hospital, Temple Street. The Adelaide's affiliation with the school lasted until 1960.[13] Each hospital paid a fee per student for the instruction received, and lectures were organised on a day release basis. The school was located at 101 St Stephen's Green, and lectures were later conducted at the Royal College of Surgeons in Ireland.[14] In addition to the instruction received at the school, Adelaide probationers also attended some evening and weekend lectures in the hospital.

Most of the gold and silver medals awarded by the Dublin Metropolitan Technical School in this period were awarded to Adelaide nurses. In 1945, the Matron, Miss Woodhouse, introduced the annual hospital examination and those obtaining the highest marks received a gold medal given by Mrs Bewley, a silver medal given by the Medical Board, and a Silver medal for the best second-year nurse given by the Chairman of the Nursing Committee.

Victoria Hospital Cork

The General Nursing Council for Ireland made provision for affiliations between two or more hospitals, which when affiliated, could be considered sufficiently large to seek approval as training schools, and the process for approval involved a small hospital seeking an affiliation with a larger hospital.[15] In 1942, the Adelaide received an application from Victoria Hospital Cork, proposing such an affiliation. The application was favourably considered by the Nursing Committee, and following a visit to Cork by the Matron, Miss MacQuillan, conditions under which applicants would be accepted into the Adelaide were prepared.[16] Applicants to Victoria Hospital would be interviewed by the Matron of the Adelaide, receive fourteen weeks' probationary training at the Adelaide, complete one year and nine months' at Cork, and complete a further two years at the Adelaide. Probationers would wear the Adelaide uniform and it was suggested that the Victoria Hospital might adopt the Adelaide uniform. Given the limited accommodation in the nurses' home, the Adelaide undertook to accept a maximum of seven probationers in any one year. In the event, some of the 'girls sent up from Cork' for interview were rejected for training. However, the arrangement began with three probationers in the spring of 1943 and a further three in the autumn, but the affiliation did not last, and in 1945 the arrangement was terminated on the recommendation of the Adelaide Nursing Committee.[17]

Later in 1948, the Victoria Hospital sought to revive the affiliation with the Adelaide, and while the Adelaide approved the application, it appears that the proposed revived affiliation did not occur, most likely due to the fact that the General Nursing Council considered the system of affiliated training schools to be unsatisfactory and sought to phase them out.

The Nursing Committee, 1920–1949

After 1920, the Nursing Committee continued to have overall responsibility for all matters concerned with nursing at the hospital. As a sub-committee of the Board of Management, it comprised medical and lay members, but had no representative from the Nursing Department. At its monthly meetings, Matron's written report was read, and on occasions, Matron was required to attend meetings. The Bewley name featured prominently in the membership of the Nursing Committee in the 1930s and 1940s, and included Dr G. Bewley, Dr H. Bewley, Mr E. C. Bewley, and Mrs Louisa Charlotte Bewley, who became one of the first women members of the Adelaide Board.[18] A prominent Dublin Quaker family, the Bewleys worked tirelessly in managing the hospital and were especially committed to its Nursing School.

The Nursing Committee had overall responsibility for decisions about nurse training. Accordingly, all decisions concerning instruction and assessments were the province of medical men and lay men, albeit with the benefit of a monthly report and advice from the matron of the day. Matters routinely considered by the Committee included the number of nurses required to staff the hospital, appointments of staff nurses and senior divisional nurses, the selection and appointment of probationers, and confirmation of their admittance to full training after the trial period. Other matters regularly discussed included nurses' and sisters' salaries, and disciplinary matters. In this connection, the Committee presided over decisions regarding dismissals of probationers, particularly those who were deemed unsuitable for training at the end of the trial period.

Difficult period

The smooth running of a busy hospital like the Adelaide depended on good working relations between the various grades of staff, and in particular, between medical staff and the senior nurses charged with the everyday running of the main clinical departments. While these working relations were generally very good, from time to time there were tensions and conflicts, and these usually occurred at the fault line that was hospital and ward administration.

In July 1939, Miss Stewart advised the Nursing Committee of 'considerable friction' between two of her very senior nurses, and later in November, when the Nursing Committee was again advised of ongoing friction between the two women, they each received a letter from the Committee advising that they should in future do their best 'to promote goodwill and smooth working in the hospital'.[19] Despite this advice, both women were again before the

Committee on foot of separate complaints of lack of cooperation on their part. Matters did not improve and Matron continued to experience difficulties in managing 'her subordinate staff', and a special sub-committee was established to consider and report on 'the nursing administration and discipline of the Hospital.'[20] The sub-committee's report found evidence of 'friction constantly occurring in the hospital', and focused attention on Miss Stewart's management and not the behaviour of her subordinates. In the light of this, Miss Stewart submitted her resignation in December 1939.[21] Her successor was Miss F. A. MacQuillan who was Matron for four years.

In 1944, Miss MacQuillan was succeeded by Miss Woodhouse, who had previously been Matron at the Musgrave Clinic in Belfast.[22] Miss Woodhouse commenced her duties in March 1945, with Miss Joynt, who had been previously the Sister Tutor, as her deputy. In April 1947, new tensions arose after some senior medical staff questioned Matron's decisions in making senior nursing appointments. Members of the Nursing Committee who were 'anxious to appoint our own nurses when possible' were dissatisfied with Matron's failure to appoint a nurse to the position of Sister, which resulted in that nurse resigning. The Nursing Committee reinstated the nurse in question. The Committee was also dissatisfied with Matron's appointment of a Sister to the Outpatient Department, without having first established her experience of theatre work. In response, Miss Woodhouse wrote that she had 'lost her confidence of the [Nursing] Committee and of the Medical Staff', and she resigned in the following June. Her deputy Miss Joynt resigned in July. Miss Woodhouse continued to enjoy the confidence of her nursing colleagues, and became a prominent member of the Adelaide Nurses' League.

The 'difficult period' seemed to end with the appointment of Margaret J. Dornan as Matron in October 1947. Miss Dornan came to Dublin with a 'magnificent record' as Matron of Guy's Hospital in London, in which role she had 'already given convincing proof of her ability'.[23] In 1948, Miss Willis was appointed her assistant. However, it appears that a residue of the tensions in the Nursing Department spilled over into the early part of Miss Dornan's tenure as Matron. In October 1948, a special meeting of the Nursing Committee was called to 'consider matters of administration', including Matron's 'increasing difficulty in the administration of the hospital … largely due to a lack of cooperation on the part of the sisters.'[24] Tensions were also evident when the Committee Chairman Dr Jackson reported that the sisters' meetings 'had produced no constructive discussion or suggestion but a series of complaints'. The Committee resolved to 'make it clear to the Matron and to the sisters that the Matron's authority was fully backed by the Nursing

Committee, who expected loyal co-operation from all members of the nursing staff.'[25]

Called before the Nursing Committee to explain the difficulties, Matron advised that there were difficulties 'in connection with off-duty lists, [and] failure to report facts of importance to her and other matters'. Eight sisters were summoned before the Committee, and the Chairman cited instances of lack of co-operation with the Matron. One sister remarked that reporting the death of a patient to Matron was not possible because she (the sister) was much too busy, and that it was not possible to plan an off-duty list owing to the present complement of staff, and with an extra sister needed. The Chairman addressed the sisters, advising them that 'loyalty and co-operation would have to be established as soon as possible … that the Matron's authority must run [and] … that the [Nursing] Committee were all loyal to the Matron and determined that she should run the hospital.'[26] It appears that after this episode, Miss Dornan's time was less fraught and that good working relations were restored.

The Adelaide nurse, 1920-1949

In the inter-war years, nurses' conditions of employment were determined by the prevailing economic situation in the country and by the local economic circumstances in each hospital. Nurses in training provided the bulk of the nursing workforce in the training hospitals, and in common with many other workers of the period, nurses' salaries were generally poor, they did not enjoy a pension scheme, and working hours were long.[27] In 1923, for example, the Adelaide probationer's off-duty time consisted of 'one half of each Sunday, morning and afternoon alternately, [and] on week days two afternoons from 3 pm to 10 pm and on 3 hours of each of the other 4 days.'[28]

By the late 1920s, clinical activity in the hospital had increased to such a high level that the Board of Management believed that the number of nursing staff, then at seventy four, should be increased. The Alexandra Nurses' Home was by then 'filled to its utmost', and as in previous times, limited accommodation for nurses placed restrictions on the number of nurses that could be employed. In 1931, accommodation was provided for an additional eight nurses and four ward maids.

In the 1930s and 1940s, selection interviews were held on three occasions in the year, March, July and November, and the number of applicants interviewed varied from approximately twelve to eighteen. While nursing shortages were a feature of the period, the Nursing Committee exercised strict selection criteria; of the eighteen applicants interviewed in November 1933, just two were accepted for the trial period, while in the following March, of seventeen applicants interviewed, just nine were accepted. Later in 1946, in response to a communication from the Irish Nurses' Organisation wishing to know whether 'the nursing profession were represented on all interview boards', the hospital advised that the system of selecting probationers at the Adelaide Hospital was 'entirely satisfactory', and that each selection committee comprised the Matron and medical and lay members of the Nursing Committee.

Signing on after the probationership trial period involved the nurse entering into a contract of employment with the hospital. While the General Nursing Council's Rules specified three years as the required period of training, many hospitals contracted trainees to give a fourth year in the service of the hospital, after which time the hospital certificate and badge were awarded. In the case of the Adelaide Hospital, the additional fourth year was in place since 1900, and the policy was reaffirmed by the Nursing Committee in 1941.

In early 1936, the Nursing Committee considered the shortage of candidates applying for training, and it introduced measures to increase the number of applicants, including reducing the age of admission to eighteen years, providing free uniforms during the first year, and reducing the educational fee to £10. A sick pay scheme for the exclusive use of Adelaide Hospital staff was introduced in 1946. Shortages of applicants for training continued to be a problem in the 1940s. After 1942, all probationers presented themselves before the Nursing Committee at the end of the trial period, and if satisfactory, were admitted to full training. However, admittance to full training was not a given, and many were 'not allowed to sign on', despite the abiding problem of maintaining the full complement of nurses to staff the hospital. Once accepted for training, the certainty of remaining in training was also not a given; the Nurses' Rules empowered Matron to 'suspend a nurse at any time for misconduct, inefficiency, neglect of duty or behaviour prejudicial to the hospital.'[29]

In instances when a nurse might be short of the requisite time to complete training, the Nursing Committee considered the circumstances which caused the period of absence. Often this was as a result of illness or family circumstances, and where the shortfall was relatively short, the Committee was generally sympathetic and awarded a certificate of training. In 1943, the Committee approved the general provision that a probationer be permitted a maximum of two months' sick leave during their four years of training.

Despite the prevailing economic circumstances of the time, the hospital endeavoured to meet its obligations to nurses as employees and to match conditions of employment that were the norm elsewhere. It the 1940s, a staff nurse or sister wishing to marry was forced to break their contract of employment and resign. In the period, the Nursing Committee was keen to have Adelaide-trained nurses in senior positions, and when such positions arose, nurses from the hospital were encouraged to apply.

Uniform and badge

The Adelaide nurses' uniform and badge have always been the most outwardly representation of the Adelaide Hospital. Mrs Louisa Bewley donated the sisters' bar and the Adelaide Hospital nurses' badge, which was struck in 1921.[30] Based on the Adelaide crest, the nurses' badge contained the Arms of the Kingdom of Saxony, which form part of the Arms of Saxe-Meiningen, the family crest of Queen Adelaide. Mrs Bewley believed that the badge gave Adelaide nurses 'a certain distinction'.

Revised Nurses' Regulations in 1936 provided for staff nurses to have a uniform distinct from that of nurses in training. The red and blue colours of the belt worn with the uniform denoted the official position of the qualified nurse; a blue belt was awarded to a nurse on becoming a state registered nurse, while a red belt was worn by out-staff. In 1947, 'distinguishing stripes for probationers' were introduced; these comprised 'one red stripe to be worn after the first year of training and two after the second, provided the probationer has made satisfactory progress in her work.'[31] The awarding of stripes brought some privileges, such as additional late passes, but additional stripes also brought added responsibilities, and it was usual for a two-stripe nurse to be in charge of a whole landing while on night duty.

Conditions of employment

In 1930, the Lancet Commission on Nursing was set up to enquire into the shortage of nurses in the United Kingdom at that time. Published in 1932, the Lancet Report revealed conflicting ideals at the heart of the recruitment problem: senior nurses emphasised the vocational ethos of nursing that they believed required nurturing through routine, strict discipline and unquestioning obedience, while more progressive thinkers saw the need to develop the nurse's critical mind, her personality and wider interests, and to promote a 'normal social life'.[32] The Commission's Report also pointed to petty restrictions and indifference to changing expectations of women at that time, and noting great variation in nurses' conditions of employment across hospitals, the Report made recommendations on nurses' hours of duty, rest periods, and holidays.[33] The Adelaide Board considered the Report and expressed satisfaction that the hospital measured up well to its recommendations:

> [We are] gratified to find that in comparison with the other British hospitals, the standard of work required from the nurses, the amount of time off duty allowed for meals and recreation, the holidays given, were surpassed by no other similar hospital. Salaries in general were somewhat lower than in England but compare favourably with other Irish hospitals … Nearly all the recommendations of the Lancet Commission for the comfort of the nurses were already being carried out under the direction of our Matron, Miss Stewart.'[34]

Miss Stewart was also trying, 'as far as possible to introduce two or three of the remaining recommendations that were approved by the Nursing Committee'.

A Nurses' Representative Council was established in 1937 to provide a forum for discussion between Matron and the representatives of the nursing staff 'on questions affecting the wellbeing of the nurses', and in 1939, a sub-committee on Nursing Services made a number of recommendations on nurses' conditions of employment, including consideration of a pension scheme for nurses, and the installation of central heating to improve the comfort of the nurses' rooms. However, the sub-committee rejected the idea of permitting trainee nurses to live outside the hospital, and recommended deferrment of a 96-hour fortnight 'until a more favourable opportunity arises to put it into force.'[35]

At that time the total complement of nurses was seventy-five, of which number, fifty-eight were nurses and probationers, eleven were sisters, and six were out staff, indicating that the hospital continued to provide nurses for private cases. However, by this time, nurse training was becoming increasingly focused on hospital nursing, particularly with the growth of medical technology.[36]

In 1943, a Matron's salary started at £120 and rose to a maximum of £150, while that of a Sister Tutor was £100, rising to a maximum of £140. A sister's salary ranged from £70 to £120, and a state registered nurse received £45. Nurses in training received a salary of £16 in first year, rising to £36 in the fourth year. Approval of salary increases tended to be made on an individual basis, and requests for salary increases required the approval of the Nursing Committee and satisfactory reports from the senior medical staff in whose department the nurse was assigned.

Nurses' health

Like her counterpart in other training hospitals in the inter-war period, the Adelaide nurse could experience poor health, with tuberculosis being a constant threat, and a number of students were forced to enter sanatoria for treatment. Dr Geoffrey Bewley conducted a study entitled *Tuberculosis in Nurses and Students,* which was published in the *Irish Journal of Medical Science* in 1942. Reporting on the incidence of TB over an eighteen-year period, he showed that the incidence and associated poor health were about four times higher among nurses than among medical students.[37] He reasoned that this was due to the fact that young men were less susceptible to infection than women and had much less close contact with infected patients than nurses.

Working in Victoria House in the period before antimicrobial drugs was particularly risky; one nurse who commenced training in 1924 lost six months of training having contracted typhoid fever while nursing there.[38] With physical fitness in vogue during the 1930s, sporting activities were encouraged; a hockey club was established in 1933, and in 1938 tennis and badminton courts were provided in the grounds of the hospital. Mindful of the realities of nurses' health and a wider recognition of workers' rights and wellbeing, in the early 1940s the hospital afforded nurses in training a maximum of two months' sick leave during their four years' training, but sick leave should not exceed fourteen days in any one illness. This fourteen-day period was later extended in 1946, but a nurse was not permitted to continue her training if a period of sick leave exceeded six months.

'The vexed question'

Despite mention of petty restrictions in nursing schools in the Lancet Report of 1932, nurse training continued to reflect the regime of custodial care and close surveillance that had obtained since the nineteenth century.[39] An article entitled 'Hospital Discipline' published in the *Irish Nurses' Magazine* in 1944 called on the student to accept discipline as a necessary part of her training and to recognise that 'submission to close supervision' was a test of her moral stability and 'her temperamental and … intellectual fitness for the career of a nurse.'[40] She should avoid 'hoydenish levity or thoughtlessness and reckless frivolity in the pursuit of some flitting entertainment'.[41] Many similar articles published in the period carried a clear message, to which all the training hospitals appeared to subscribe.[42] Writing in the *British Journal of Nursing* in 1946 the Matron of Charing Cross Hospital in London remarked:

Regarding the vexed question of discipline, I find very few of the present-day trainees resent reasonable discipline, but many when they have left and gone to hospitals where discipline has been relaxed, have disliked it intensely, and have then realised the value of having been trained in an atmosphere of discipline. Discipline is necessary for any communal life and for any highly skilled training, so why belittle it? We all need discipline in our youthful days and until we have learnt to discipline ourselves.[43]

Not everyone subscribed to this view, and attitudes and practices in the training of nurses were being questioned. In 1943, one Irish doctor commented that a probationer 'must submit to stricter discipline than a girls' school'[44] and later in 1948, an Irish parliamentarian remarked that the harsh regime for a nurse in training was 'bound to have some effect on her nervous system, some effect on her outlook in life'.[45]

Discipline was seen as a way of forming a young girl's character for the demanding work of nursing, and accordingly, the training hospital acted *in loco parentis* to the trainee. In the years 1920 to 1949, discipline and close surveillance remained strong features of a nurse's training experience at the Adelaide School. Students' parents were frequently written to in matters concerning the academic progress and discipline of their daughters. A formal letter from the Chairman of the Nursing Committee was the customary way that a sanction or reprimand associated with a breach of discipline was communicated to a nurse. Reprimands were issued for a variety of offences committed in the course of ward duties, including 'being rude to a patient' and 'unseemly behaviour with a male patient in the ward'. In 1948, a nurse was deprived of her stripes for three months for being untruthful in saying that she had prepared a patient for theatre when she had not. Reprimands also resulted from breaches of rules relating to leave. In 1935, one nurse was suspended for three months for 'insubordination and being out when she should have been in bed, as she was on night duty'. In the event, the period of suspension was reduced to one month on foot of a letter of apology from the nurse's father. Another nurse was suspended for six months for having 'overstayed her dance leave for 2 hours, returning to the hospital at 4.15 am and coming in by an unorthodox route'.[46]

Restrictions on nurses' recreation time were a feature of the period; under revised regulations in 1936, nurses were required to be in at night at 10 pm, with lights out 'half an hour after the nurse is due in', and staff nurses enjoyed an additional hour at night to 11 pm. Later in 1938, special permission was granted to staff nurses to have 'dance leave to 2.0 am not more than once a month', and in 1947, the arrangements for leave passes were again revised, permitting red and blue belt nurses to have passes until 11 pm and dance passes, with Matron's permission. Second, third and fourth year nurses were permitted a late pass until 11.15 pm once a week, and a dance pass till midnight, and first year nurses were expected to return to the Nurses' Home at 10.30 pm each night, but could have a late pass 'occasionally'.

While romantic liaisons between nurses and doctors are the subject of popular fiction, such liaisons were also a reality of hospital life, and the Adelaide Hospital was no exception. However, if conducted in a way that was seen to transgress hospital rules, such liaisons could result in a nurse getting into trouble with the hospital authorities. In 1937, one nurse was found by Night Sister to be sitting on a resident pupil's knee at 1 am in No 5 Ward. She was duly suspended, but having 'admitted the offence and apologised' to the Nursing Committee, she received a reprimand and was permitted to return to work after one week. Although contact between nurses and medical students was 'greatly frowned upon', many Adelaide nurses married Adelaide doctors.

Finding fault

The quality of the training experience greatly depended on the quality of instruction that the senior nurses gave and the quality of interpersonal relationships between trainees and their instructors. Such relationships could be fraught and, from time to time, the probationer could find herself the hapless subject of a severe and demanding instructor. Ward sisters could be among the severest and most demanding, although a trainee had recourse to plead her case if she felt her instructor was too harsh.

Maureen Woods, who entered the Adelaide in 1945, remembered her training as 'tough and disciplined', and she recalled the ward sisters, including sisters Crawford, McDermot and Douglas, who 'reigned supreme on Landings 1, 2 and 3', and Sister Acton who reigned in Victoria House.[47] Sisters who had a reputation as being strict and demanding tended to be remembered in retrospect with fondness for their excellent teaching.[48] Sister Acton was remembered as someone who was very strict and junior students anticipated going to Victoria House with much trepidation; one former student wrote:

[In Victoria House] for the first week nothing we did was right ... she would take each one of us aside and say, 'You're all right now, I think

I've knocked all the nonsense you learned on the landings out of your head.'[49]

While she was considered very strict, by the end of training, she 'was almost a friend', and many students grew fond of her.[50]

Despite reigning supreme, even very senior members of the nursing staff could be the subject of the opprobrium of the Nursing Committee. In 1940, one senior sister appeared before the Committee to answer the charge that complaints had been received about her 'severity to the nurses ... of not listening to any excuse and of generally making life unpleasant for them, so much so that ... having regard to this [girls] have preferred to go to England for training instead of coming to the Adelaide.'[51] Later in 1944, the Nursing Committee received a report from Matron that another senior sister was 'not teaching the nurses under her', and having considered the matter, the Committee concluded that the sister 'was finding fault more than giving positive teaching', and cautioned her that she would have to resign if further complaints were brought against her.[52]

Cleanliness, Christmas and other memories

Maureen Woods remembered first arriving 'up the stone back stairs' to the nurses' home, and being shown to her 'dark and dingy' small cubicle. She also recalled the daily inspections of bed pans and urinals in the sluice room by Matron on her rounds.[53] Lily Nuzum, who entered training in 1946, remembered her training as being very hard work, especially sluice room duties.[54] She also recalled how Sister Joynt, the Home Sister, was so 'fussy about ... cleanliness in the nurses' home'. Known as 'Ball and Socket', Sister Joynt was also remembered as someone with 'a good brain, and better still, a sense of humour'.[55] Gertrude Jeffers, who commenced training in 1949 and later became Night Sister, also remembers the emphasis on strict cleaning, with one ward sister going down on her hands and knees to inspect underneath the four-legged bath and demanding that the bed frame be thoroughly washed each time bed making was performed. Like many students, having to perform the routine to the absolute satisfaction of the ward sister seemed ludicrous, and the situation in which she found herself caused her to react with uncontrollable laughter:

> [Having] washed the wheels and frame [of the bed] for the third time, I could contain my laughter no more and was unable to get up off my knees and continue ... I wondered what sort of mad house I had come into! Sister didn't quite see it that way and immediately ordered me to

go to Matron's Office, and see if she was amused! Although Matron kept a straight face, I left with the impression that yes, she too saw the funny side.[56]

Christmas time at the Adelaide in the 1940s was remembered as 'a most wonderful time'. Gertrude Jeffers remembers the large Christmas tree in the main hall, carol singing and lanterns, Sister Crawford leading a train of carol-singing nurses through the wards, and Sister Daisy McDermott giving out the 'refreshments' all around on request. Medical students were always mischievous, particularly at Christmas time, and Maureen Woods recalled one Christmas Eve, when a group of students got a donkey into the lift and rode it around the wards.[57]

Maureen Woods also remembered how the doctors and surgeons were held 'in high esteem and reverence'. Similarly, Lily Nuzum recalled how students had to respect their seniors, including the senior medical staff; in the case of one senior surgeon, nurses were expected to open the door for him 'without a please or thanks' as he entered and left the ward. Deference to one's superiors was carried across all grades and within the body of nurses and nursing students; hence a very junior student learned quickly that there was a 'pecking order', which meant standing to one side to let a more senior nurse pass and not taking one's seat in the dining room until the more senior nurses were seated.[58] She also remembered night duty, when 'you'd go home and sleep ... [a] whole two days, you'd be so tired, and night duty in summer months with open windows, and feeling hungry as the pleasant smell of biscuits wafted in from the Jacob's Biscuit Factory across the street. On one occasion during the summer, she had to present herself for night duty all red 'like a lobster', having fallen asleep in the sunshine on the roof of the nurses' home.

The Emergency

In 1939, just twenty years after the disaster of the Great War, a new war in Europe was yet again having an impact on the Irish economy and on the Adelaide Hospital. At the commencement of the war, the hospital was adapted as a casualty clearing station in the event of hostilities spreading to Ireland, and a number of the hospital's nurses gave service in the War. These included Kathleen Griffiths ARRC, who was posted to a casualty clearing station in Iraq and later to Malta and Sicily, Phyllis Noblett, who served with the Queen Alexandra's Imperial Military Nursing Service (QUAIMS) in the 90th British General Hospital in Malta and later in Benghazi, and Gladys Tyndall

RRC, who was present at the fall of Singapore. Gladys Tyndall was also posted to Belgium where she took charge of the British General Hospital, and she was later involved in setting up the first hospital in Bergen-Belsen to care for the survivors of the concentration camp following its liberation in April 1945. After the war, she was elected President of the Adelaide Hospital Nurses' League from 1950-1954.

When Phyllis Noblett commenced training in 1940, Nurse Mary Cooper was a staff nurse on Landing 2.[59] Mary Cooper (QAIMNS) joined the Queen Alexandra's (QAs) in 1940 and was on service in the Far East when she was captured by the Japanese and imprisoned along with other QAs at Palembang in Sumatra. In October 1942, her Japanese captors assigned Mary and three fellow QAs, Margot Turner, Jenny McAllister and Olga Neubrunner, to work for a period in a local hospital run by Dutch and Indonesian doctors.[60] The four were later returned to prison in Palembang, where Mary and her fellow POWs experience harsh and cruel treatment at the hands of their captors. Mary died in prison and was remembered in a Hospital Memorial, an Oak Credence Communion table, presented by Mrs Louisa Bewley.[61] Her fellow prisoner Margot (later Dame) Turner survived to become Director Army Nursing Service (DANS) and later Colonel Commandant (CC) of the Queen Alexandra's Royal Army Nursing Corps.[62]

Hospital surgeon Mr Somerville-Large served with the RAMC for six years in the Middle East, Mr Grantham gave service in the RAF, and Mr Kinnear served with the British Red Cross. Like Gladys Tyndall, Mr Kinnear also served at the Bergen-Belsen camp and on his return to the Adelaide gave talks and slide shows on the concentration camp.

The most immediate impact of war on the hospital were the price rises and shortages of certain goods, including foodstuffs like fish and cereals, drugs, and especially fuel, which necessitated rationing of coal, which in turn curtailed heating of the hospital. In 1941, a special appeal for support was made, and events were organised, including a gymkhana and social and sports events, yielding an additional £500 in 1942. In addition, Matron's Pound Day Appeal raised almost £800 and nearly a ton of 'produce' in that year. The Linen Guild was also particularly active at the time of the Emergency, procuring stocks of bed linen, night attire, and slippers for patients.

The savings made on non-replacement of fuel and drugs, due to their limited availability, led to budgetary improvements, in the short term at least. The salaries of nurses were increased in 1943 and again in 1945, and new pay and sickness and superannuation schemes were introduced for some staff.

These additional costs were offset in part by monies donated by the Dublin Hospital Sunday Fund, which amounted to over £1,800 in 1945, and by the £1,100 raised by Matron's Pound Day appeal in 1946.

The ending of the war in 1945 did not bring immediate relief; fuel had almost doubled in the final three years of the war. However, with the dark clouds of global conflict passing, the Adelaide Hospital and its Nursing School could look to a brighter future. Students who trained during this period experienced the deprivations of poor wages and few luxuries. Lily Nuzum remembers how, having queued up for the 'little brown envelope' at the end of the month, the monthly salary was soon spent on a trip to the Green Cinema on St Stephen's Green, followed by something to eat, and the purchase of a pair of black stockings.[63]

Adelaide Hospital Nurses League

The Adelaide Hospital Nurses League held its first meeting on 8 November 1946. Miss Woodhouse welcomed the members of the new League, which duly elected its first officers and drew up its Constitution. Alice Reeves RRC was elected President, E. G. Barrett RRC, Matron of the Merrion Nursing Home and a member of the Adelaide Board of Management, was elected Vice-President, and Miss M. E. Joynt, Assistant Matron, was elected Honorary Treasurer.[64] The Honorary Secretary was Miss Marie Crawford, and the ordinary members of the Executive Committee were Miss Power and Mrs Richardson. At the time of its founding, the register of members listed 101 names that included nurses who had trained in the last decade of the nineteenth century. Miss Woodhouse and Mrs Louisa C. Bewley were each elected honorary members. Miss Woodhouse later married and, as Mrs Ervine, was made a life member of the League in appreciation of her services to the Adelaide Hospital and for the active part that she had played in founding the League in 1946. Mrs Bewley later became Patron of the League.

The League's objective was to 'form a bond of union between past and present nurses and to encourage them to maintain a high standard of work and conduct and to promote mutual help and social intercourse'.[65] Part of the impetus for establishing the League was the fact that Adelaide nurses did not have a pension scheme, and through its Benevolent Fund, the League aimed to support nurses who were not married and therefore did not have the support of a husband.[66]

The League quickly became active in the everyday life of the hospital. Within a decade, membership of the League had doubled to well over two hundred, and in 1959 the first international branch of the League was established in Scotland, and branches were later established in London, British Columbia, and Northern Ireland. The President's medal was struck in the early 1960s. The League's first Annual Dinner was held in 1960, at which Miss Emily McManus CBE was the guest of honour.

Eight members of the League's Executive Council were represented on the National Council of Nurses of Ireland, a body that was affiliated to the ICN. The League also sponsored one of its Executive Committee to travel to international meetings of the ICN to countries like Sweden, Switzerland, Germany, and the United States. The League grew its members over the years and produced a comprehensive annual report, detailing the League's activities, reporting on former Adelaide nurses, giving notices of births and marriages, and publishing obituaries. Each annual report carried a matron's report giving updates on developments in the hospital and the Nursing School.

Meetings of the League were generally held in the Adelaide Boardroom, and aside from the formal business, it was usual to have a guest speaker, followed by a visit to the hospital and the nurses' home. In its early years, the League undertook fundraising activities for the hospital, including sales of work, in order to improve conditions for patients and promote nursing and nursing education at the hospital. One of the earliest benefits was the establishment of a hospital trolley shop.

The Nurses' League celebrated its fiftieth anniversary in 1996. Today the League remains active, has over seven hundred members and continues to play a prominent role in the Adelaide Hospital Society.

CHAPTER SIX

Hard collars and crossover belts: The Adelaide School, 1950-1979

In 1950, An Bord Altranais (the Nursing Board) replaced the General Nursing Council for Ireland as the regulatory body for nursing and midwifery. Dr Noël Browne, the Minister for Health who established the Nursing Board, wanted to ensure that recruitment and training of nurses took account of the wider needs of the health services and not just those of individual hospitals.[1] However, he did not wish to interfere with the 'internal arrangements' of the voluntary hospitals that had a good record in training nurses. While the voluntary hospitals were required to make some changes to the course of instruction and provide modern training facilities, they continued to act as independent institutions, recruiting their nurses and conducting nurse training according to their own particular needs.[2]

Being wholly self-financing and dependent on charitable donations and endowments, the Adelaide Hospital remained independent of direct state control, and in this connection, it continued to experience the challenges of maintaining its services. As in previous decades, the annual grant made by the Dublin Hospital Sunday Fund was an important source of income; by 1950 the sum donated by the Fund and other parish collections amounted to around £4,000 per annum. Like many other similar-sized hospitals in Dublin in the period, the Adelaide featured in the state's plans to develop acute hospital services on a more rationalised and efficient basis. Moreover, the hospital's position of independence from state support was growing increasingly difficult to sustain as it continued to develop as a modern teaching hospital with new specialist services in areas like cardiology and neurology. The advent of Penicillin in the late 1940s and other new drugs and new healthcare technologies meant that patient turnover and clinical activity were increasing, resulting in inevitable rises in day-to-day costs. The challenge of financing the expanding services was so great that the hospital was forced to end its independence from state financing in 1960.[3]

This period saw the passing of some notable Adelaide staff. Marie Crawford, who had been a ward sister for thirty years, died in 1954. Sister Crawford entered the Adelaide as a probationer in 1920, having previously been a VAD serving from 1916-1918. She became the Sister on Landing 3 in

1927 and there had found her 'true vocation'. She was remembered as the 'ideal sister', and was renowned for her excellent teaching skills and her willingness to give her time to probationers. She became the President of the Nurses League on the year that she died. In sickness 'her only anxiety was to get back to her beloved landing as soon as possible.'[4] Number 16 Ward on Landing 3 was named the Marie Crawford Ward in her honour and the Marie Crawford Memorial Fund was established. In 1964, Dr Augusta Young, a consultant dermatologist and former nurse at the Adelaide died, and in the following year Mrs Louisa C. Bewley, the Patron of the Nurses' League and the first lady appointed to the Adelaide Board, died. Students fondly referred to Mrs Bewley as their 'fairy godmother' when on special occasions in the dining room she supplied éclairs from the Bewley family restaurant on George's Street.[5] Sister 'Daisy' McDermott, for many years the Sister on the Men's Landing and later Assistant Matron, died in 1977.

The Adelaide Hospital, 1950-1980

A modern hospital would make for a more efficient hospital, and in 1949 the Adelaide acquired a new boiler, a new refrigeration room, and a new physiotherapy department. In 1950, it acquired a new x-ray developing room and new operating theatre, containing a modern sterilising plant, and new bathrooms were installed in 1951. When full electrification was completed, electrical storage heaters were introduced throughout the hospital, making the 'noisy coal bucket and dirty ash pan ... a thing of the past'.[6] Amid all this modernisation, a new little chapel with a 'serene atmosphere' was constructed in the old boardroom. The chapel was described as 'very simple, but lovely', with light oak paneled walls and blue velvet curtains. The Adelaide Nurses' League provided the Chair for the Chapel Sanctuary.

These developments inevitably impacted on the hospital's financial position, and the annual budget for 1949 showed a deficit of £14,000. Despite the 'gloomy' financial picture, the hospital treated almost 2,400 inpatients and more than 44,000 outpatients in that year. The financial position remained precarious throughout the early 1950s, and the need for extreme measures to address the deficit were only averted by successful fundraising initiatives, including the Matron's Annual Pound Day Appeal, the Shilling Fund, the Adelaide and Fetherstonhaugh linen guilds, and the Adelaide Campaign, which was instituted by Seymour Leslie, the Appeal Organiser appointed in 1948. The Matron's Pound Day was one of the more successful fundraising campaigns in this period; in 1954 over £2,000 was raised, and for her efforts Miss Dornan was 'warmly praised by the Board for her assiduity'. However, the modernisation project that it had embarked on in this period had placed the hospital in so precarious a position that it was forced to appeal directly to the government for financial assistance in 1955. After 'considerable negotiation' with the Department of Health, a capital grant of over £40,000 was secured, marking the beginning of the end of the hospital's full independence.[7]

Further advances in medical science, better clinical facilities and a widening of health service provision after the Health Act of 1953, led to greater activity in the hospital's clinical departments. As activity grew, the needs for extra space and equipment grew, and in the late 1950s plans were prepared for a new extension to accommodate the orthopaedic and X-ray departments. Also planned were an extension to the nurses' home and additional accommodation for medical students, which was needed following the introduction of medical internship training. The Matron's Pound Day appeal provided necessary funding – in excess of £3,500 – to permit interim improvements in the overcrowded nurses' home; new beds and curtains, improved lighting, and a new heating system were installed in 1958. Anticipating the costs of the planned extension, a General Building Appeal Fund was established in 1959 and within a year over £20,000 was raised. A programme of building began in 1960 that included the new Featherstonhaugh Wing, which comprised two new wings in the former Victoria House, interior rebuilding of the radiology and pathology departments, and modernisation of the main entrance hall.

Despite the success of fundraising for new building developments, the day-to-day costs of running a busy modern hospital treating almost 3,000 inpatients and 60,000 outpatients annually, continued to rise, and in order to meet its running expenses in 1960, the hospital was left with no alternative but to accept financial assistance from the government through the Hospitals Trust Fund. Government funding was made through a daily capitation grant that, in return, required state-funded hospitals not to charge a fee for public patients. By 1969, the daily capitation rate per patient was 15 shillings. However, the hospital continued to rely on fundraising, charitable donations and legacies in this period.

The Dublin Hospital Sunday Fund ceased to operate in 1960. The Fund's long association with the Adelaide Hospital, which began in 1876, was important in times of financial difficulties, and the annual grant made by the Fund had come from the proceeds of public donations. With the demise of the Fund, a new Adelaide Hospital Sunday Fund was established, with the assistance of members of the former Fund, and in subsequent years, monies donated by the Adelaide Fund went to provide facilities for patients, such as a radio system for the wards. After this period, the traditional fundraising schemes continued to operate, including the Linen Guild, the Matron's Pound Day Appeal, and the Shilling Fund. The Adelaide Nurses' League was also active in fundraising. Charitable fundraising events included the annual Midsummer Fair and the annual concert given by the Trostan Singers choir, founded by Molly Dunlop in about 1953.

'The Feds'

In 1959, the Adelaide was one of seven Dublin voluntary hospitals, which included the Meath and National Children's hospitals, that came together to discuss proposals to establish a federation of hospitals. During discussions with the then Minister for Health, Sean MacEntee, to consider the necessary legislation to achieve such a federation, the Adelaide sought assurances that owing to the 'exceptional position' in which its Charter had placed it, any contemplated legislation should contain special provisions to ensure its original objects would be preserved. In the event, the legislation to establish the federation retained the Adelaide's essentially Protestant character within the federation, including the full autonomy of its nursing school.[8]

The new Federation of Dublin Voluntary Hospitals, or the 'Feds' as it was generally referred to, brought benefits to its member hospitals, including the pooling of pathology, hospital maintenance, and clinical supplies services. Under the Federation, the Adelaide established a new Neurological Diagnostic Unit in 1962. Later in 1965, the hospital established an intensive care unit, the first of its kind in Ireland.

A concern for the Adelaide Board of Management in this period was the government's future plans for the development of acute hospital services in Dublin. In 1968, there were plans to break up the Federation and establish a new large centralised hospital at St Kevin's (later St James's) Hospital. Further changes were contemplated by the Board when the Health Act of 1970 established eight new regional health boards in Ireland, and a new national body, *Comhairle na nOspidéal*, to approve the appointments of hospital consultants. These new public administration structures were viewed as a threat to hospitals like the Adelaide, since they represented a trend to replace voluntary lay people with civil servants in the management of public voluntary hospitals. The Board of Management expressed this concern in its Annual Report of 1970, referring to 'the trend of ... state control', which was likely to make remove 'the incentive of all those voluntary workers on whose support this hospital has relied so much since its foundation.'[9]

Adelaide nurses 1895
(Courtesy of the
British Library)

Theatre, 1903

Adelaide uniform,
c. 1900

Nurse Meta
Armstrong, c. 1910

Fever Hospital

Fetherstonhaugh
Convalescent Home

Adelaide nurses 1914

Nurse Emma Palmer,
c. 1904

Sister Eleanor Dixon
1896

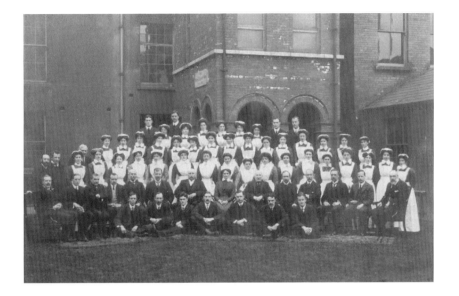

Miss Hill Matron and Adelaide staff, 1910

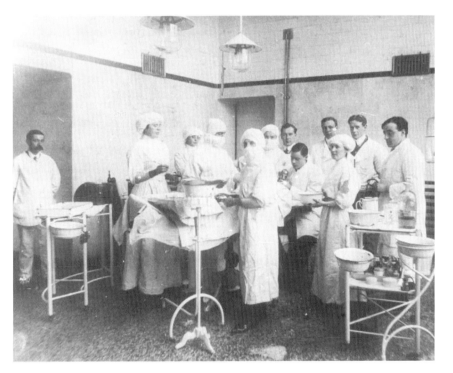

Theatre, 1923

Interior Alexander
nurses' home sitting
room

Interior Alexander
nurses' home dining
room

Queen Victoria visits
the Adelaide Hospital,
1900

Nurses McIntosh &
Young, 1910

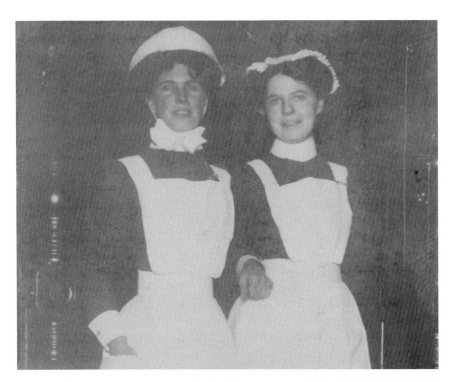

Sisters Burkitt &
Swaine 1911

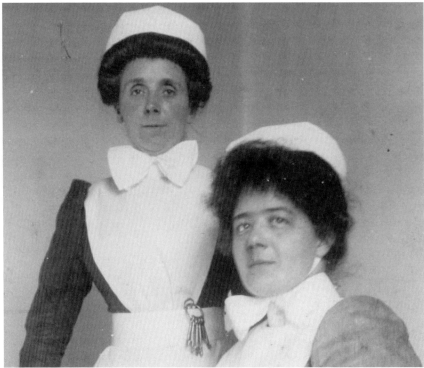

Children's ward,
c. 1904

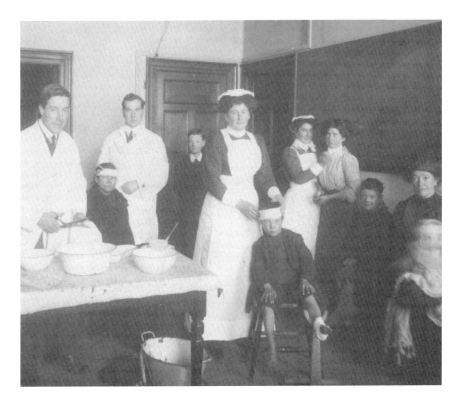

Nurses and doctors
bandaging children,
c. 1904

The Brooke Ward,
nurses Bayliss and
Adams 1910

Farnham Ward c.
1910. Nurses Johnson
and Holman with (L
to R) patients Dean,
Kelsall and Hudson.
Ernest Dean is pic-
tured here with a
broken tibia sustained
while playing rugby
for the Adelaide
against Oxford
University. He was
later killed at Loos in
1916 serving with the
RAMC.

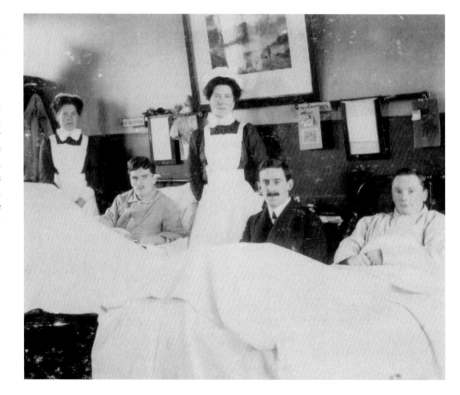

Kathleen (Kitty)
Brewer, 1934

In the nurses' home,
1934

Kathleen Lynn

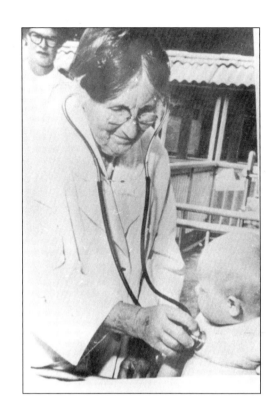

Alice Reeves
(Courtesy of the
RCSI)

Miss Stewart, Matron, and nursing staff, 1933

Miss Woodhouse, Matron and nursing staff, 1946

Nurses relaxing, 1935

Group Lord Mayor
Alfie Byrne visits the
Adelaide, 1956. Miss
Dornan is second left.

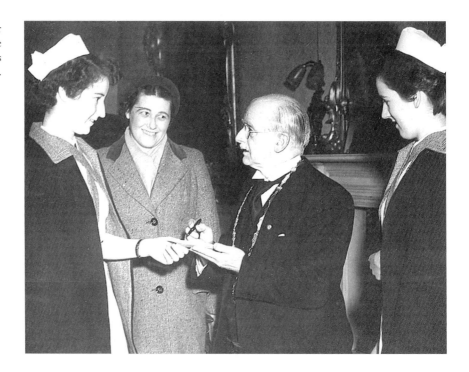

Despite these winds of change, by 1972 the hospital's recently completed programme of modernisation and its improved financial position gave the Board of Management confidence in the Adelaide's future preservation 'as a distinct entity'.[10] Additional clinical services were developed in the 1970s, including neurology, thoracic surgery, cardiology, and intensive coronary care, funded largely by charitable donations and fundraising.

Developments in the Nursing Department, 1950-1970
A perennial concern for the Nursing Department was the shortage of space in the nurses' home, and in 1951 the Schoolmaster's House of St Patrick's Cathedral was acquired as a nurses' residence to provide accommodation for eleven night nurses, giving 'seclusion and absence of disturbance ... during the day'. Alterations to the nurses' diningroom and the sisters' room were also undertaken in that year. In 1956, the long standing arrangement with the Dublin Metropolitan Technical School for Nurses was ended, and all lectures for nurses were held within the hospital after that time. This decision was brought about following the establishment of An Bord Altranais when individual hospitals were given added responsibility for giving instruction. The decision was greatly helped by an anonymous donation of £1,000, which provided modern teaching equipment and a dietetics kitchen.

The centenary of the Adelaide at Peter Street and 'one hundred years of nursing' was marked in 1958 with a special service at St Peter's Church, conducted by the Rev R. H. ('Dickie') Dowse, the Hospital Chaplain. The Lord Archbishop of Dublin preached the sermon, and the service was afterwards followed by tea in the hospital, which was hosted by Miss Dornan, the sisters, and nurses.

Margaret Dornan
Margaret Dornan retired in 1962, having served as Matron for fifteen years. She was been previously the Assistant Matron at Guy's Hospital under Miss Emily P. McManus, one of England's most celebrated Irish matrons, and she and Miss McManus remained close friends.[11] Miss Dornan always proudly boasted that she evacuated Guy's Hospital to the country at the onset of the Blitz.[12] She was especially remembered for her work in developing the Adelaide School, in which she oversaw the consolidation of all teaching at the hospital after the link with the Dublin Metropolitan Technical School for Nurses was ended. She believed that lectures given in the hospital by the doctors and surgeons in their own 'special subjects', would give the students a

'better understanding of the work being done in the wards'. At the time, many of the doctors' lectures were conducted in the Boardroom.

Miss Dornan was lauded for her unsparing devotion to the welfare of the hospital and her high standards, 'which she considered so essential', and she was especially noted for her skills as a brilliant organiser of fundraising. She considered herself as a colleague of medical staff, and they, in turn, respected her as an equal. She was also concerned for the welfare of her nurses; while a student Joan FitzPatrick remembers how Miss Dornan insisted that her (the student's) dentist perform a dental extraction in the Adelaide theatre, as she did not want her nurses sitting in some dentist's chair.[13] She was later remembered as a regal lady, who was 'very strict' and called herself 'the Queen of the Adelaide.'[14] Her regal claim was no doubt justified by her appearance in her Sister Dora cap, which seemed to be made of 'royal material [that] shimmered on her head' like a crown.[15] At a time of considerable international debate about nurse training, Miss Dornan's parting remarks to the Adelaide Nurses' League was to call on them to ensure that the Adelaide School should 'continue to exist in spite of all the changes'. As a Scottish woman, she loved Scotch whisky, and she retired to her beloved city of Edinburgh in the mid 1960s, where she later died.

1960s

In what was by now something of a tradition in the appointment of a new Adelaide Matron, Miss Dornan's successor Miss Deirdre de Burgh was recruited from one of the great London voluntary hospitals, in this instance, St Thomas's Hospital. A native of Naas, Miss de Burgh's arrival coincided with the building of the new extension to the nurses' home. Completed in 1964, the new accommodation included a new sitting room, fitted out with soft furnishings of the highest quality, and Miss de Burgh and the nurses were 'very pleased with their new quarters and most appreciative of the extra comforts'. Additional teaching accommodation was also provided at that time, when two nurses' dining rooms were converted for use as classrooms. Nevertheless, lack of sufficient accommodation for nurses remained a concern, and plans to address this involved the provision of a new doctors' residence at 21 Peter Street, thereby releasing space for an additional fourteen nurses' rooms.

Deirdre de Burgh's time as Matron coincided with the Lemass Era, a period of economic growth in the early 1960s that led to improved conditions of employment for nurses, with improved salary and shorter working hours. In the late 1950s, a first year staff nurse earned just £12 a month. A strike by nurses at St Kevin's Hospital in pursuit of better pay resulted in improved salaries in the early 1960s, and nurses' conditions of employment were further improved with the introduction of an 80-hour fortnight for staff nurses.[17] Miss de Burgh retired in 1966 and was remembered as a matron who had brought a more modern outlook to nursing at the Adelaide. She believed that if the Adelaide wished to keep its school at the forefront of developments then it should have 'an open and receptive mind to new ideas and methods'.[18]

Maureen Campbell, also a former nurse at St Thomas's Hospital in London, was appointed her successor, but remained as Matron for little more than a year, and in 1968 Marjory R. Douglas was appointed Matron. A sister at the Hospital for twenty-five years, Miss Douglas was held in high esteem by both staff and patients, and her appointment was widely welcomed. As Ward Sister on the Children's Ward, it was her custom to save money for the poorer local children, and she always ensured that, when discharged, they were provided with new clothes and food. She was also remembered as a 'very strict' matron who could be 'very cross', and Yvonne Seville recalls her earliest encounter with her. When asked to give her name and having replied 'Yvonne', Miss Douglas took her by the arm and said: 'Indeed! … I don't want to know what your mother called you; I want to know your name, your surname!'[19]

At the time, the practice of morning and evening lectures was in place and attendance was compulsory, even while on night duty. However, Miss Douglas presided over the full implementation of the 'block system' for organising classroom instruction. Other developments at this time included the introduction of clinical placements at other hospitals, including St Brendan's Psychiatric Hospital and the Royal Victoria Eye and Ear Hospital. At the time of Miss Douglas, forty students were recruited each year in two intakes of twenty and recruits were drawn from both city and rural areas. Classroom instruction was conducted by Sister Tutor Perry. Sister Perry was also Matron-in-Charge at the Sunshine Home in Leopardstown.

Judith Chavasse

Sister Perry was joined in the School in 1963 by Sister Judith Chavasse, who returned to the Adelaide having completed the nurse tutor diploma course at University College Dublin. Sister Chavasse was previously the Sister-in-Charge on the male orthopaedic ward on Landing 2.[20] Like many former senior Adelaide staff, she trained at St Thomas's Hospital in London, and as a staff nurse at St Thomas's, worked with Deirdre de Burgh, who was then a Ward Sister.

After the introduction of the nurse tutor diploma at UCD in 1960, the title 'sister tutor' was gradually replaced with 'nurse tutor'. As a nurse tutor, Judith Chavasse became active in nursing affairs, attending many international meetings, including the Congress of the ICN in 1965 in Frankfurt. Sister Perry attended the same Congress as the representative of the National Council of Nurses in Ireland. At a time of considerable international debate about the apprenticeship training system, Miss Chavasse was a regular contributor to debates in professional journals. Commentating on the training system in 1968, she suggested that the advantage of apprenticeship training in small schools like the Adelaide was that it fostered 'maturity and responsibility' ... [and] strong corporate bonds' among students.[21] However, she recognised that the reality of apprenticeship training was that 'inevitably routine patient care takes priority over educational ideals.'[22]

When later reflecting on her experiences as Night Sister at the Adelaide, she commented on the potential risks and the real challenges of running a hospital staffed mainly by students, particularly during night time hours; in 1960 the total complement of night staff at the Adelaide consisted of the Night Sister, just one registered nurse, and students in training, including first year students. Night duty for students involved twelve-hour shifts, with five nights off in a month, and as Night Sister, she herself recalled having to work twenty-nine consecutive nights. It was not unusual for a second year student to take charge of a ward of more than twenty patients while on night duty, and night duty in Victoria House was particularly difficult, as it involved a single student working on three floors without a lift and each morning having to empty and clean the sputum mugs of the many patients with TB.[23] At the time Sister Perry was concerned that very inexperienced junior students were placed on night duty and she worked to end the practice.

Born in Cork, the daughter of a clergyman, Judith Chavasse grew up in Oxford and trained initially as an orthopaedic nurse at the Wingfield Morris Hospital in Oxford and later at the Nightingale School at St Thomas's. She recalled the grandeur of St Thomas's, with the 'enormous, greater than life-sized' statue of Florence Nightingale in the front hall with a little vase of flowers always kept fresh in front of it'. She particularly remembered that the Nightingale School was characterised by 'the weight of history and tradition' and the 'tremendous reverence' provided for Miss Nightingale, a reverence which some students did not always hold, and in lighter moments, mockingly referring to her as 'Holy Flo'.

When she first came to the Adelaide in 1959, Judith Chavasse took up a position of staff nurse at the Victoria House, before becoming Night Sister and later Sister-in-charge on Landing 2. On her return to Ireland, she was struck by the parochialism of Dublin, where personal contacts were important in conducting public affairs; for example a patient admission to the Adelaide could be arranged by a telephone call from a clergyman. She was also struck by the level of extreme poverty in Dublin at the time, particularly in the area around the hospital; as a sister in orthopaedics, she attributed delayed fracture healing to the low-protein diet that poor people were accustomed to. Having worked in the more 'egalitarian' milieu of St Thomas's, she was also struck by the expectation of total obedience to doctors by nurses, and the fact that nurses and ward sisters addressed consultant staff as 'Sir'. She attributed this subservience less to the historical distinction of gender and class and more to the 'educational distinctions' of the time, when the nurse was 'not generally considered to need academic qualifications equal to that of other ... caring professions.'[24]

Judith Chavasse believed in the distinct contribution of the nurse to patient care and she particularly valued the nurse's autonomy in decision-making at the bedside. While practising this principle, she sometimes found herself crossing swords with medical staff, who could misconstrue her assertiveness and questioning attitude as a challenge to their self-perceived absolute clinical authority. She brought many ideas about nursing from St Thomas's and before taking up Miss Dornan's offer to undertake the tutor diploma course at UCD, she requested that she defer her place for one year in order to implement new methods and approaches that she had learnt at St Thomas's.

She remembered with fondness some lighter moments, including the time that she was the subject of a prank when some mischievous students placed 'L' plates on her motorcycle. As a ward sister she availed of the bottle of Guinness, supplied daily by the Guinness Brewery as a privileged afforded to sisters who needed it for medicinal purposes. However, her daily supply was quickly withdrawn when it was discovered that she ordered it because she simply liked Guinness! One of the duties of a ward sister was to keep careful count of ward stocks, such as thermometers and ward cutlery. Her approach in this regard was pragmatic; rather than having to report a missing spoon and give a full explaining of the circumstances of it going missing, she purchased two spoons in Weir's of Grafton Street to have in reserve, just in case a spoon disappeared. In the event, she had recourse to use one, but retains the other to this day!

In 1967, Judith Chavasse obtained a BA degree, and in 1969 after ten years at the Adelaide, was appointed Director of the Department of Nursing Studies at University College Dublin. In that role, she developed the nurse tutor diploma as the first nursing degree in Ireland. She went on to become one of Ireland's most prominent nursing leaders, and throughout the 1970s and 1980s was at the forefront of the major developments in nursing education in Ireland. She was well known and highly respected among her peers and students alike. In retirement, Judith Chavasse continued to take an active interest in nursing affairs and went on to complete an MPhil degree at Queen's University Belfast and, in 2004, she was awarded an Honorary Doctorate from Trinity College Dublin for her 'outstanding contribution' to the development of nursing and midwifery in Ireland.

Training experiences, 1950-1979

Throughout the period 1950-1979, new thinking on the training of nurses was emerging, and at international meetings of the ICN, the WHO, and other fora, there were frequent calls for the separation of nurse training from hospital nursing service.[25] The system of hospital training was seen by many as too narrow and monotechnic to meet the needs of the nurse of the future. These same ideas were also being debated in Ireland, and a study into nurse training conducted in the late 1960s indicated dissatisfaction among Irish student nurses with their training.[26] Commissioned by the Irish Matrons' Association, the study revealed that although students valued their ward learning, they were dissatisfied that classroom instruction and ward learning were not well integrated, and they also complained that little time was set aside for private study.

Despite concerns about the quality of training at the time, nursing remained a popular career choice for young Irish female school-leavers.[27] The number of applications for training places in the Adelaide School far exceeded the number of places available. While the curriculum was gradually expanding to accommodate new material that reflected new skills and new nursing roles, much of what the student experienced in training had changed little since the earlier part of the century. The training experience during the period 1950 to 1980 was recalled by a number of former Adelaide nurses who gave oral testimony.[28]

Uniform

Most students remembered their first day on arriving at the Adelaide, and having to cope with the new uniform with its 'belts and all the pins for the aprons and the awfully hard collars ... and the cap which had to have five pleats.' The cap was a particular challenge on the first day, since the wearer was presented with a flat piece of material, which somehow had to be transformed into a hat with its 'wonderful five flutes at the back'. Fitting the dress was no less challenging, as one former student remembers: '[it had] a detachable collar, which needed a stud ... an apron, which needed to cross over and ... which had a crossover belt, and then you ... had to attach that with big safety pins, and then you had another belt ... and then you had white cuffs to put on!' When new, the uniform could be ill fitting, and for the new self-conscious PTS who presented at breakfast on her first day in her new uniform, she could 'stand out like a sore thumb'.[29] Once the difficult task of getting the uniform on was complete, there were other challenges, not least the prospect of a uniform inspection by Matron. Miss Dornan took particular interest in the way the uniform was worn:

> Miss Dornan did a round every day and the uniform had to be below your knees and ... if the uniform wasn't below your knees she'd tell you she could see your popliteal spaces. "Nurse!' she'd say in a Scottish accent, 'your popliteal spaces are showing!'[30]

With its numerous component parts, it was described as 'a bitty uniform', and nurses 'complained bitterly about all the layers around their waist and all their aprons and never having enough aprons and people ... taking other people's aprons out of the laundry.' While the Adelaide uniform was considered 'old fashioned', nurses liked it and wore it with pride. Its distinct navy blue with white hail spot set the Adelaide nurse apart from other hospital staff and from nurses in other hospitals. Respect for and pride in the uniform was seen as pride in nursing, and on prize giving day, as one former matron recalls, nurses 'looked very spruce' as they had taken extra care in preparing the uniform on that special day.[31]

Ward and classroom instruction

In first year, training in the Preliminary Training School (PTS) involved a combination of classroom and ward instruction, and the PTS period lasted for six months, ending when the next intake of students arrived. Students were assigned to ward duties from 7.30 to 9 am and attended classes from 9.30 to 5 pm. PTS students were assigned to morning ward duties in groups of three per ward, and each student rotated through the tasks of cleaning the sluice room, cleaning patients' bedside lockers, and assisting with patient washes, which students considered to be the more skilled and more valued of the three tasks. In the 1950s and 1960s, each PTS student was supplied with a small wooden butter box containing 'rags … a bottle of disinfectant, a tin of Dando … a little brush to scrub out the bedpans and the urinals … a pair of rubber gloves, [and] a bar of carbolic soap'. After the ward report, the student was set to clean bathrooms and toilets, and to clean patients' lockers and bed tables. This cleaning was inspected by the ward sister whose careful eye and finger were used to judge the quality of the work. Daily cleaning of ward furniture and beds was also the responsibility of the PTS student. One former student remembers how in the hospital structure, the PTS held the lowliest place and could find herself subjected to the ire of a ward maid who was often more highly regarded in the hospital structure. During the mid-1970s, the monthly salary for a first-year student was £120, and aside from the morning duties during PTS block, students were also required to work on Saturday mornings from 7.30 am to 1.15 pm.

Ward work was characterised by routine and by tasks that had to be completed, and learning this routine was an essential part of the training experience at the Adelaide. Junior students greatly relied on experienced senior students and on staff nurses to help them learn particular tasks. Routine tasks included bed bathing, 'back treatments', which involved rubbing the area with methylated spirits, and giving green soft soap enemas, administered to every preoperative patient using rubber tubing. In the time before pre-packed clinical consumables, the nurse in training learned how to prepare and pack wound dressing materials, work which was undertaken at weekends, and to administer intravenous fluid or blood using glass bottles and rubber tubing. Another skill to be learnt was the preparation of morphine injections, which involved crushing morphine tables using two sterilised spoons and dissolving the powder in sterile water. Students learned how to prepare nutritional drinks, such as 'eggnog' and beef tea, and learned the importance of knowing how well each patient was eating during mealtimes and of providing assistance to those who needed it. Nutritional drinks such as Bender's Food were common, and patients with TB were given a daily 'snipe' of Guinness, supplied by the Guinness Brewery.[32]

The ward work was remembered as hard and tiring, and could involve lifting heavy patients, an especially difficult task at a time before lifting aids were introduced. Nursing patients with spinal TB demanded a lot of extra careful handling. Rotation to the operating theatre could be daunting, but the adjustment was made easy by kindly theatre staff like Joe Carroll, the Theatre Attendant, and Sister Rowe, the Senior Sister, who was remembered as friendly and was liked by the students.[33] Aside from learning some of the skills of theatre nursing, theatre duties included sewing sponges on the theatre sewing machine at weekends.

A record of each student's clinical training was maintained in the 'schedule for training', and individual clinical tasks like oral hygiene, the care of pressure areas, bed bathing, and in more senior years, wound dressings, removal of sutures, administering medicines, and so forth, were recorded in the schedule. Once completed and recorded, each task was marked and signed by the ward sister on a weekly basis, and each week Matron reviewed the schedule. A student was summoned to Matron's Office in the event of any omissions in the schedule or any queries on Matron's part. A nurse could also be summoned by the Matron in the event of having broken a thermometer. 'Shaking in [her] shoes' and with a shilling in hand to pay for a replacement thermometer, the nurse was expected to give a full account of how the thermometer got broken. Aside from the schedule of training, a report on the student's progress was written by the ward sister after a six-week rotation, and this was also presented to Matron. Students were graded as either 'good', 'fair' or 'bad', and a bad report was feared, since it also resulted in a visit to Matron.

With a good report at the end of the first three months and having passed the examination after PTS training, a nurse was permitted to 'sign on' for full training. A single stripe was earned at the end of first year and an additional stripe was added after second year. Having stripes had real benefits, since those with one or two stripes were 'less murdered' than the first year students who were 'always in trouble, always murdered, not just [by] the sisters and the staff nurses, but [by] the [student] nurses above [them].'[34] On passing the final examinations and having attained state registration, the white belt was replaced with the black belt. Since a 'two-stripes student' had already gained experience in taking charge of a ward, by the time the black belt was first worn, the transition from senior student to staff nurse was rather smooth.[35]

Classroom subjects in PTS training included anatomy, physiology, nursing skills, first aid and invalid cookery, and during second and third year, topics included medical and surgical nursing, and ethics. Classroom instruction included lectures given by doctors, physiotherapists, and dieticians. Each doctor's lecture was followed up with a tutorial on the topic of the lecture given by the sister tutor, Sister Perry. Dr Bewley, who gave medical lectures, was remembered as a 'very balanced man', whose motto was 'moderation in all things'. Classroom instruction could be fun. On one occasion, when Sister Perry mistakenly listed the bones of the arm while displaying the leg bones of the skeleton, Valerie Houlden, a self-confessed 'bit of a giggler', was sitting in the front row and in a fit of the giggles caught Sister Perry's attention. Sister Perry asked 'How old are you?', to which Valerie replied 'I'm seventeen.' Also seeing the funny side, Sister Perry replied 'Oh, I suppose you're very young.'[36]

Later in the 1970s, medical and surgical registrars gave many of the lectures. Hilary Marchant was Principal Tutor during this period and was assisted by Yvonne Seville, the Clinical Tutor, who later became Matron. Miss Marchant was remembered as a 'great tutor' for her progressive teaching methods; at a time when teaching was still very traditional, she gave students opportunities to discover new knowledge for themselves through project work and visits to other health care and voluntary agencies. She went on to hold senior positions in Irish nursing, including Deputy General Secretary of the Irish Nurses' Organisation and Assistant Education Officer with An Bord Altranais, and she was always remembered as an innovative educator, an advocate for nurses and midwives, and as a warm gentle woman of great character and intelligence.[37]

Examinations and prizes

School examinations were taken at the end of PTS training and also following periods of block instruction in second and third year, and state examinations, including the Preliminary and Final examinations, were usually taken at a central venue, such as the Examination Hall of University College Dublin on Earlsfort Terrace. The Preliminary examination had oral and practical components; the practical component involved the demonstration of skills, such as preparing an enema or removing sutures. Final examinations included written examinations, and doctor's oral examinations also formed part of the State final examinations until the end of the 1970s. Mock oral examinations were an integral part of the preparation for the state finals.

Passing the state finals brought state registration and for many a position as a junior staff nurse, or 'black belt', at the hospital. As a black belt, the nurse remained under the contract of employment that was signed at the end of PTS training, and once the term of the contract was completed in about nine months after state registration, the junior staff nurse was awarded the red belt and received her hospital certificate and badge from Matron. During the 1970s certificates and badges were presented to each individual nurse in Matron's office without formal ceremony. However, recipients of gold and silver medals attended the annual prize-giving ceremony where medals were presented alongside the prizewinning medical graduates from the Trinity Medical School. Medals were awarded for excellence in a combination of academic and practical work, and in this period, medalists included Naomi Elliott, Ruth Hipwell, Shirley Lockhart, Irene Hendy, and Sarah Condell. In 1982, the Rosse Memorial Medal, in honour of Lord Rosse, was awarded for the first time to Iris Gordon. In subsequent years Rosse medalists included Susan Laird (1982), Audrey Fennell (1983), Ruvé Stewart (1984), and H. Wellwood (1985).

In the Nurses' Home

Adapting to life as a new student at the Adelaide could be challenging. For those who had not attended boarding school, and particularly those who attended a mixed co-educational secondary school, the impact of entering the nurses' home seemed like entering a girl's boarding school, and a number of former Adelaide nurses vividly recall the culture shock of the restrictions experienced on first entering training. During the period 1950 to 1980, student accommodation consisted of six separate cubicles per room, which were part-itioned with either curtains or wooden panels – those with wooden panels were referred to as 'horse boxes'. This dormitory-like arrangement, along with the fact that students were monitored for punctuality at breakfast, added to the boarding school milieu, and for those who found themselves marked late on three occasions and deprived of leave, the culture shock must have been very great indeed.

The nurses' home was a place of rest from the long hours of work, since day duty usually ended at 9 pm and resumed the next morning at 7 am, with a 6 am alarm call. It was also a place of refuge, where relief from the tensions of work and study could be found, and hence the nurses' home was a place of fun and mischief-making. Popular pranks during the 1950s and 1960s included making apple pie beds, placing hard dried peas into a bed, and stuffing the practical room mannequin named 'Adelaide' into a student's wardrobe, from where it would fall out on top of the hapless student when she opened her wardrobe door.

Rhoda Rolston, who trained in the early 1950s, remembers pranks such as subjecting a fellow student in full uniform to a cold bath and plastering one student to another with Plaster-of-Paris, and on one occasion, Brilliant Green was poured into the uniform tub in the laundry, after which a horrified Miss Dornan was confronted with students in pale green aprons as she conducted her customary uniform inspection.[37] Medical students also delighted in carrying out pranks; once they removed the grandfather clock from the main hall and placed it on the roof of the nurses' home. On another occasion, they acquired a mannequin from Switzer's of Grafton Street, dressed it in a nurse's uniform, suspended it from the banister in the main stairway, and called Matron to inform her that one of her nurses was hanging from the ceiling.[39]

Many nurses regularly overstayed their late passes and returned usually via the window of a nurse's bedroom. The bedroom of one nurse was used with such frequency as the route of entry by late returning nurses that the occupant had grown so accustomed to the late night traffic that she slept soundly throughout![40] Nurses would hide in a laundry basket, and on many occasions almost gave themselves away by uncontrollable giggling while Night Sister locked the door. Students went to great lengths in the cause of true love. Making it home to bed to get just one hour's sleep before being called for duty could involve bribing the night porter with a few cigarettes, making one's way through a door behind a bed in Ward No 5, and emerging into the dormitory through a wardrobe door.[41] Climbing the outside fire escape in the dark in a long strapless evening dress and high heels was another option when a late pass was exceeded. The risks of being caught returning late by an unorthodox route were great; suspension of 'spring leave' could be the student's fate, and this was not good if state examinations were imminent.[42] 'Secret parties' were held in the nurses' home, and since many students entered training immediately on leaving secondary school, the first party to take place was on the occasion of the Leaving Certificate results.

Christmas remained a special time at the Adelaide in this period. Religious services in the hospital chapel and carol singing were central to the celebrations. Another Christmas tradition was the 'nurses' den' or 'Bonne Bouche', a room set aside on each ward which was decorated to function as an elaborate sitting room full of 'goodies', in which ward staff could take time out to relax, pull crackers and wear silly hats.[43] The Christmas pantomime was traditionally performed by the set in block in December.

Also reflecting its religious character a Hospital Christian Fellowship was established in 1965 and Bible study meetings were held on a Monday evening after duty in the staff nurses' sitting room. The Fellowship provided a forum of support and a mechanism for meeting with colleagues more senior and more junior in the hospital, and members also met with Christian workers from other hospitals.

Change

During the late 1970s, nurses in Ireland were concerned about a range of issues, such as their professional position, staffing structures, a lack of a clear definition of the nurse's future role in the health services, and deficiencies in the system of nurse training.[44] A Government Working Party examined these concerns, and in its Report of 1980, it recommended that student nurses' commitment to providing hospital service should not be permitted to interfere with their learning. The Report implicitly called into question aspects of the nurse training system in Ireland, especially the pedagogical quality of the training system.

At the time when the Working Party Report was being prepared, the Adelaide Hospital anticipated significant changes in the structure of the nurse training course that were the result of new European directives on the training of nurses. Introduced in 1979, the directives required every training hospital to provide additional hours of classroom instruction and additional clinical training experiences in such areas as maternal and child health, children's nursing, home nursing, and nursing in the care of older people. Like most hospitals of a similar size, the Adelaide could not provide the specialist clinical experiences stipulated by the new regulations and was obliged to negotiate with other Dublin hospitals to secure places for its students. For the Adelaide and other training hospitals at the time, the changes also necessitated the employment of additional staff nurses, since students' availability for nursing duties in their own training hospital was now somewhat curtailed.

Plans

In the late 1970s, Dublin had eleven acute hospitals, and the government's plans for hospital services envisaged a smaller number of larger hospitals through amalgamations. As members of the Federation of Dublin Voluntary Hospitals, the Adelaide and Meath hospitals were becoming more closely identified with each other, through sharing medical and other services.[45] In 1976, a Joint Liaison of the Adelaide and Meath boards was established to consider 'how best to co-ordinate the medical services of the two hospitals within [the] Federation in association with Trinity Medical School, while retaining the identities of the two hospitals and that of their nursing schools.'[46] The Adelaide's association with the Meath was further strengthened in 1977 when the two hospitals signed a joint declaration 'expressing their willingness at some future date to move to a new major hospital'. With this association, the Adelaide Board foresaw 'a glimpse of a new dawn ... visible on the horizon', and a visit by the Minister for Health in 1977 was seen as an important sign of the government's interest in the hospital and its future. In that year, the government announced plans to develop a third major hospital for south Dublin at Tallaght, of which the Adelaide and Meath would 'form the nucleus.'[47] The common future of the Adelaide and Meath came a step closer in 1978 when the two hospitals accepted an invitation from the Minister for

Health, Charles Haughey, 'subject to certain safeguards', to join together in planning the new hospital.

At that time, the Adelaide Board was determined that the planning for the new hospital would not detract from its core objectives 'to maintain and develop our medical skills, our Nurse Training School and our traditional high standard of patient care.'[48] The Board predicted that the time leading up to the proposed move to Tallaght would be 'potentially very difficult', and while its future lay alongside the Meath Hospital, it was determined that the Adelaide should 'remain strong and ... keep pace with modern practice'.[49] The Board Chairman, Mr D. Graeme-Cook, wrote of the need to build the staff of the two hospitals, not in a competitive but in a complementary way, and he observed that the excellent track record of the Adelaide Nursing School would be important in assuring its future, 'in whatever modified form', in the government's future plans for nursing schools in Ireland.

CHAPTER SEVEN

From 'the dear old Adelaide': The Adelaide School, 1980-2009

At a time of anticipated change, the Adelaide Hospital was at its most active, treating in excess of 5,000 inpatients and over 35,000 outpatients, a doubling of the numbers of twenty-five years previously. While a relatively small hospital, the Adelaide was progressive in the field of medical science; in 1979 it established a Research Foundation for medical research, and within a year, sufficient funds had been raised to permit the Foundation to award its first research grants.

In 1980, Miss Douglas resigned and her deputy Eileen Mansfield was appointed Matron. With a background in military nursing – she was a former QA nurse – Miss Mansfield had worked at the Edinburgh Royal Infirmary and was also the former Night Sister at the Adelaide. She quickly established her position and was the first matron to publish a Matron's Report in the hospital's Annual Report. In her first report she remarked that the training of nurses had become 'more difficult and complicated', given the necessity to comply with the new European directives on the training of nurses, which brought additional classroom and specialist clinical instruction.[1] In this period, the school was also responsible for in-service training to prepare qualified nurses for their role in training students. With just two tutors in 1980, Mary McCafferty and Avril Shaw, the work of teaching almost 120 students was demanding, and the expanded training programme necessitated additional nurse tutors.[2] In 1983, Miss McCafferty, who succeeded Hilary Marchant as Principal Tutor, took two years' leave to work in Bahrain as a Nursing Officer and Avril Shaw was appointed Acting Principal Tutor. Miss Shaw was assisted by new tutors Barbara Lennon and Joan FitzPatrick and by clinical teacher Susan Laird. The tutors worked closely with their counterparts at the Meath and the National Children's hospitals in planning for a proposed amalgamated nursing school at the new Tallaght Hospital. At that time, the school obtained a new study room, an expanded practical room, and painting and rewiring were also completed.

The economic difficulties of the mid 1980s touched the hospital, when many of its trained nurses found it difficult to obtain employment, and this time was marked by emigration of nurses to countries like England,

Australia, the United States, and the Middle East. Despite the national 'cut-backs' in health spending, the hospital continued to provide a full service, and in 1984 it increased the number of patients treated. Following the closure of Dr Steevens' and Sir Patrick Dun's hospitals in this period, the hospital took on additional surgical, nursing, administrative, catering and house-keeping services.

Even through the very difficult years of health service cutbacks, the hospital continued to promote continuing education for its qualified nurses and funded numerous specialist clinical courses, seminars and study days. With an eye to the future, the hospital also sponsored a small number of its nurses to undertake the nurse tutor degree course at University College Dublin. The Adelaide tradition of resilience in the face of adversity remained strong throughout the difficult years of the 1980s, and the solidarity of its staff in this adversity was particularly evident at that time.

In the period, the deaths took place of a number of the hospital's long-serving Board members, including Mr Edward C. Bewley, Dr Geoffrey Bewley, Mr Henry M. Hall, Mr R. J. Walker, and the Earl of Rosse. In 1986, the Canon R. Dowse Adelaide Scholarship was instituted to commemorate the memory of the hospital's chaplain of longstanding, who died in 1983. Later, in 1992 Lord Iveagh, Vice-president for many years, died.

In 1980, the hospital was granted an amended Charter, which rationalised 'previously accepted departures' from the 1920 Charter's rulings and which brought it up to date for the circumstances in which it now found itself. This amended Charter was later amended in 1996 to become the Charter of the Adelaide and Meath Hospital incorporating the National Children's Hospital, and was the vehicle that permitted the Adelaide ethos to continue in the new Tallaght Hospital.

In planning to move to Tallaght, the Adelaide authorities continued to negotiate with the government about its future status. In the years between 1979 and 1993, these negotiations became fraught at times, but the hospital was 'absolutely determined' to retain its place as part of the Trinity Medical School, its Nursing School, and its particular traditions that were seen as 'central to its future'.[3]

Retaining the tradition
The Tallaght Hospital Board was established in 1979, and the new hospital comprised the Adelaide, Meath, and National Children's hospitals. The Board met for the first time in 1981, bringing 'an element of reality' to the situation for the Adelaide Board.[4] A project team of the new Tallaght Board,

which included the matrons of the three constituent hospitals, was appointed to begin planning for the new hospital, and liaison committees met regularly to co-ordinate medical, nursing and administrative functions of the three hospitals.

With the establishment of the Tallaght Hospital, the Adelaide Board was determined that the 'high standard' and 'unique ethos' of the Adelaide should be maintained in the new hospital, a position that was motivated not by a desire to be separatist, but by 'partnership' and a 'democratic spirit', and in 1982, the Adelaide Board adopted a number of objectives that included the following:

> To honour the specific objectives and legal obligations laid down in the Charter with special reference to preservation of the Protestant ethic [and] to preserve and enhance the quality and prestige of the Nursing School.'[5]

The Adelaide Board held that the constitution of a new Tallaght Hospital was contingent on 'certain assurances' from the government that would enable 'the continuation of the Nursing School and its ethic' and it secured such assurances in 1984 when the Tallaght Board agreed to retain up to forty student places annually to ensure the continuation of the Adelaide School.[6] The agreement was approved by the Minister for Health, Barry Desmond, and was supported by An Board Altranais (the Nursing Board).[7] Graham Patrick Moss, the Chairman of the Tallaght Hospital Board, set out the Adelaide's position in relation to its wish to retain the Adelaide School:

> The [Tallaght] Board of Management believes that it is essential that the special position of the Adelaide School of Nursing in the eyes of the Protestant community be retained [and that] … due recognition be paid to the different ethical approaches to nursing between Protestant and Roman Catholic nurses … In order to avoid undue ethical pressure on some nurses, the Board deems it necessary to protect an ethos and ethical code which does not find [certain medical] procedures repugnant. This can only be achieved if some schools take positive steps to ensure that the proportion of Protestant nurses is sufficiently large to merit separate ethical lectures and to guarantee the continuation of that ethic into a genuinely pluralistic interdenominational hospital.[8]

The Adelaide Board was 'well pleased' with the agreement and believed that it provided 'the necessary guarantees for the future.' Plans for the new

Tallaght Hospital moved a step closer when architects were appointed in 1985.

Added anxiety: the CAB

In 1986, the Nursing Board set about establishing a national Central Applications Bureau (CAB) with the aim of assuring national consistency and uniformity in the recruitment and selection of nurses.[9] While a laudable idea in principle, the initiative was not welcomed by the health boards and the voluntary hospitals. Since student nurses were hospital employees at that time, hospital managers held that it was their prerogative to select their own employees, and would not countenance a system that would effectively remove that prerogative. The Adelaide Hospital was adamant that the special position of its Nursing School would be maintained in any revised arrangements, and in common with many voluntary hospitals, it strongly opposed the proposed centralised system. The Adelaide authorities were determined that the responsibility for selecting nursing candidates should remain with individual hospitals, and hoped that 'all those whether parents, clergy or teachers to whom potential Protestant nurses will turn for advice, will treat this determination as a most serious undertaking on the part of the [Adelaide] Board of Management.'[10]

The hospital made representations to the Nursing Board expressing its concerns in the matter, but in March 1987, the new CAB was constituted. Its establishment was, in Miss Mansfield's words, a cause of 'considerable anxiety' to prospective recruits to the Adelaide School.[11] However, while the establishment of the CAB had the force of legislation, the strength of opposition from so many quarters was such that the fledgling Bureau never took to the wing, and after less than six months, the Nursing Board abandoned the Bureau.

New uncertainties

Having met the leaders of the four main churches in 1989, the then Prime Minister Charles Haughey gave assurances that he wished to see the Adelaide ethos represented in the new Tallaght Hospital, and in the following year, the Minister for Health, Rory O'Hanlon, spoke of the government's commitment to enabling the Adelaide ethos 'continue as an integral part of the public hospital system.' These assurances notwithstanding, there was wider public concern that the Adelaide tradition should be preserved, and the Protestant community gave voice to this concern in the public media and in parliamentary debates. Public support for the Adelaide position from within and outside the Protestant community gave the Adelaide Board confidence that the hospital was well positioned to preserve its nursing school, its 'liberal traditions', and its links with the Protestant community in Ireland.

Minister O'Hanlon established a Working Group 'to consider possible future management arrangements' for the new teaching hospital, its nursing school, and 'the position of the Adelaide as a focus for Protestant participation in the health services'.[12] Chaired by T. D. Kingston, the group proposed that the new hospital should be managed under an amended Adelaide Hospital Charter, be named the Adelaide Hospital, have its President nominated by the Adelaide, have a shared chairman among its constituent hospitals, and have an ethical code based on privacy in the patient-doctor relationship. The Adelaide Board accepted the Kingston proposals 'after much soul searching', but the Meath Board did not and it proposed amendments that were, in turn, not acceptable to the Adelaide Board. The failure to get agreement resulted in some tensions between the Adelaide and Meath boards.[13] However, the Adelaide Board remained confident that the government would fulfill its commitment to preserve and nurture the Adelaide's 'unique position as the focus for minority participation in health care'.[14]

The difficulties were exacerbated in 1992 when the government moved to revise its policy on the size of the new hospital and its role as a teaching hospital, and instead of funding the building work, referred the project to an independent committee.[15] This development led to suggestions that the Meath Hospital alone would move to Tallaght, that the National Children's Hospital would amalgamate with Our Lady's Children's Hospital, and that the Adelaide would remain at Peter Street. At the time, newspapers carried reports that 'the Adelaide has been saved', but the Chairman of the Adelaide Board declared that 'nothing could be further from the truth [and] the future of the Adelaide is in the balance', and he wrote that the Adelaide could no longer remain at Peter Street:

> The premises, the dear old Adelaide, are indeed too old and too small to be a proper independent modern teaching hospital well set to care for patients well into the 21st century.[16]

These difficulties were compounded by renewed financial problems in 1991 and 'the grave situation' ended the optimism of just a year previously. A visit by President Robinson to the hospital in July provided only temporary respite from the gloom. The situation became critical in 1992 when the government reduced the hospital's budget, resulting in rumours about the hospital's future existence and fears of large scale staff layoffs and of the hospital's ability to remain as a viable teaching hospital for medical and nursing students.

At the time the Adelaide Board feared that the government was attempting to close the hospital through under funding, and it seems that these fears were not without foundation. At one point in 1992, the hospital was asked to withdraw from the Tallaght project, but it remained steadfast in its belief that an alternative development would be impossible and that Tallaght was the 'best solution to the Adelaide's future.' Reflecting the mood of the Protestant community that the Adelaide was 'being edged out of the hospital system', Dr Robin Eames, Archbishop of Armagh, remarked: 'We are an angry people.' The anger was compounded when the Minister for Health Dr John O'Connell announced a decision to proceed with the Tallaght project in late 1992, but failed to invite any member of the Adelaide Board to the official ceremony to announce the decision. The Adelaide saw its treatment at the hands of the government as part of a wider question, 'that of government against people', and as a threat to all voluntary sector involvement in public healthcare.[17]

Resolution

An end to the uncertainty was evident in January 1993 when a new coalition government took office, and announced that building work on the new Tallaght Hospital would commence in 1994. Good relations between the hospital and the government were restored, but the Adelaide Board remained concerned that the ethos of the last remaining teaching hospital associated with the Protestant community in the state, should be 'maintained in an identifiable and secure way'.[18] Further public meetings to support the Adelaide were held in Dublin and Wicklow in early 1993 and the large attendances attested to the level of public support for the Adelaide cause. In April, the Chairman of the Adelaide Board, Professor McConnell, was invited to address Mass-goers at Castleknock in Dublin, and having set out the Adelaide position, was generously applauded by the congregations attending.[19]

The future of the Adelaide had a symbolism far beyond the immediate matter of the composition of the Tallaght Hospital Board. At the time, the peace process was beginning to take root in Northern Ireland, and the way that the Irish government handled the Adelaide's future would tangibly demonstrate its commitment to ideals of tolerance, inclusiveness, pluralism, and of embracing all traditions on the Island of Ireland.[20] Hence the Protestant community on the whole island viewed the Adelaide cause as emblematic of their cause in a new post-conflict Ireland.

The years of uncertainty were finally ended in 1993 when 'resolution of the major difficulties' surrounding the management structure of the new Tallaght Hospital was achieved under the Minister for Health, Brendan Howlin. Devised by a Working Party of all stakeholders,[21] the resolution lay in the constitution of the new Tallaght Board and in an agreement that guaranteed 'the place of the new hospital as a focus for Protestant participation in the health services, while confirming freedom of conscience and the free profession and practice of religion by all within the institution.'[22] Under the agreement, the new Adelaide and Meath Hospital, incorporating the National Children's Hospital would be multi-denominational and pluralist and governed by an amended Adelaide Charter, retaining 'the particular denominational ethos' of the Adelaide. The Tallaght Board would comprise six representatives each from the Adelaide and Meath hospitals, three from the National Children's Hospital, and two government appointees, and its new *ex-officio* President would be the Church of Ireland Archbishop of Dublin, who would also nominate six Board members.

At the time the Adelaide Board acknowledged the widespread support for the Adelaide position from all sections of Irish society, and the Board's Chairman Professor McConnell remarked how the Adelaide cause was 'sympathetically and ... enthusiastically adopted by people of all walks of life, from all sections of society, and across the whole island.' He also thanked 'our friends in the Liberties [who] spoke for us when it really mattered' and he contrasted the hospital's 'extremely dangerous position' of 1992 with its assured future in 1993.

Adelaide Hospital Society
With the newly constituted Tallaght Hospital Board, necessary legislative modifications were needed to the Adelaide Hospital Charter to enable it to become a vehicle for managing the new hospital. It was also necessary to consolidate the Adelaide Hospital Society as a way of supporting the new hospital, so that 'the minority community [would] be able to continue to participate fully and actively and in a major way in medicine in Ireland [and] in particular, the ethos of trusting medical and nursing staff to behave ethically but without ethical preconditions.'[23] The Adelaide Hospital Society would become a Charitable Company and be the nominating body for six members of the Tallaght Hospital Board.

The Society appointed a new Director, Dr Fergus O'Ferrall, and among his first tasks was to prepare the text of the Tallaght Hospital Charter. When the wording of the new Charter was agreed and finally ratified in 1995, the legal and constitutional arrangements were in place for managing the new hospital and these were finally passed into law in 1996. Dr O'Ferrall's appointment was seen as an important factor in 'rejuvenating' the Adelaide Hospital Society, and under his directorship, the society played a key role in facilitating the practical expression of the Adelaide ethos in the years of transition from the old to the new hospital.

Planning for change: nursing services and the Adelaide School
As the time to move to Tallaght drew closer, the consolidation of services between the three hospitals continued, and the Meath, Adelaide and National Children's (MANCH) group of hospitals was established as the organisational umbrella for planning for the relocation of services to Tallaght. Adelaide student nurses were placed in the Meath and National Children's hospitals for clinical experiences, and this was seen by Miss Mansfield as a way of helping to 'draw the MANCH group closer together.'[24] She recognised the importance of providing student nurses with the full range of clinical experiences commensurate with the role of nurses in a modern hospital. Classroom teaching was also shared among the three hospitals, and Miss Mansfield believed that this co-operation was not just based on the need for more 'logical and … economical use of resources', but was also aimed at 'making nursing of the highest quality'.[25]

In 1989, the hospital celebrated the 150th anniversary of its founding at Bride St. This was marked by a number of events, including a Service of Thanksgiving at Christ Church Cathedral in May, a musical evening at the National Concert Hall, a dinner at Trinity College, a Masked Ball at the Mansion House organised by the nursing staff, and the publication of David Mitchell's commemorative history *A Peculiar Place*. Marking the Adelaide's tradition of public service to the sick poor, these celebrations were given added significant in a year that saw the hospital experience the full impact of the financial 'cutbacks', which necessitated the closure of thirty beds for the entire year. At a time when there was a growing demand for acute hospital services, it was ironic that the financial challenges that marked its first year should again be visited on the hospital in its anniversary year.

Bruising and bewildering time
Miss Mansfield described 1989 as 'a bruising and bewildering time' and she questioned the real cost effectiveness of government policy in cutting acute hospital services, since, many patients not admitted to hospital due to limited bed capacity would eventually be admitted in a deteriorated condition.[26] She

also expressed concern that the crisis in the health services was adversely affecting recruitment into nursing by making the profession seem less attractive to prospective applicants. Also of concern was the impact that the reduced number of acute medical and surgical beds was having on the nurse training programme; with fewer beds, fewer clinical cases could restrict learning opportunities for students. This necessitated students having to undergo some of their training in other hospitals, and Miss Mansfield calculated that well over two-thirds of a student's three-year training time was being spent in hospitals and services outside the Adelaide. This was also related to the European directives that required a wide range of clinical training experiences. Nevertheless, Miss Mansfield saw the learning value of such external clinical placements. In her Annual Report for 1989, she looked to the future with determination and optimism:

> With the year 2000 approaching … we are determined to keep up the standards and ideals of the Adelaide. We face the next few years with the confidence that we are doing good work.[27]

In the early 1990s, with her counterparts at the Meath, the National Children's and St James's hospitals, Miss Mansfield began discussions with representatives of Trinity College Dublin and the Nursing Board on proposals for a degree in nursing. The initiative had come from the Tallaght Planning Group, and Miss Mansfield recognised that a degree in nursing would in the future become the major route of preparatory training for nurses. These discussions continued into 1993, but moves were already afoot that would alter the entire landscape of nurse training in Ireland and would render the discussions with Trinity as redundant at that time.

Eileen Mansfield

Despite the Adelaide authorities' hope that she 'might prove everlasting', Miss Mansfield retired in March 1992 after twelve years as Matron. She had 'vividly represented the true spirit of the Adelaide and her daily presence on the wards … [would] be sorely missed', and the Adelaide Board's Secretary, Rosemary French, paid tribute to Miss Mansfield:

> As a Matron she was unique. She was feared, respected and very much loved by all her staff and patients and her devotion and loyalty to the hospital and her staff was outstanding. The hospital revolved around her.[28]

The Board Chairman, Professor McConnell, also paid tribute to Miss Mansfield remarking that she was 'probably the best known and best loved matron in Ireland … [whose] advice was sought, and freely given, all over the country.'[29] She 'ruled the Adelaide with a unique mixture of strong discipline and good humour … [and] was a stickler for standards in all respects', and all Adelaide staff knew this.[30] She was noted for her grip:

> Her 'grip' was notorious – she would approach with a jolly smile, grip you by the biceps and squeeze quite painfully until you agreed to some very reasonable request – money for a scheme to make patients more comfortable or to provide better training for nurses, or any of a hundred different schemes she had under way for the good of the hospital.[31]

Miss Mansfield came to the Adelaide in 1969, and as Matron, she held many senior appointments, including membership of An Bord Altranais and the Dublin Hospital Initiative. Her colleagues in the School of Nursing remembered a matron who strongly supported their efforts to develop nursing education for the future, and who recognised and respected their skills as educators.[32] As one former Adelaide tutor remarked: '[the] working relationship between the nursing administration and the school was very much one of [mutual] respect – administration respected education and education respected administration and the [nursing] service.'[33] Another tutor observed that Miss Mansfield 'saw the value of education and professional development for [nurses and] it appeared as if she never said 'no' [and] … was very skilled at identifying the potential in people.'[34]

Behind her rather stern exterior, Miss Mansfield had a sense of humour and delighted in sharing a joke or an innocent prank with her senior colleagues in the nursing department and the school. She also enjoyed a tot of whiskey from time to time. Her motto was 'remember the patient comes first', and on retiring she remarked that 'with the modern age of technology … common sense and communication must continue to prevail if there is going to be a happy hospital for the benefit of the patients.' Eileen Mansfield died in 1998 and did not live to see the opening of the Tallaght Hospital. The Eileen Mansfield Scholarship was established in her honour, and continues to be awarded to nurses by the Adelaide Hospital Society.

Miss Seville

Miss Mansfield's successor was Mrs Aileen Henderick, and reflecting the new times, she carried the title of Director of Nursing and Matron. However, in the following year Mrs Henderick left the Adelaide to pursue postgraduate studies at Trinity College.[35] Yvonne Seville was appointed Matron in 1993, a critical period for the hospital and its nursing school. She had been Assistant

ADELAIDE HOSPITAL.

DUBLIN

This is to Certify that *Adelaide Elizabeth Hayes* received practical and theoretical training in the **Medical & Surgical Wards** of this Hospital from 1st September 1910 to 8th December 1944 that her conduct throughout has been satisfactory and that she is duly qualified to discharge the duties of a trained nurse.

S. F. MacQuillan MATRON *J. K. Hopkins* CHAIRMAN OF NURSING COMMITTEE

Issued 8th day of December 1944

Adelaide Nurse's certificate, 1944

ÁRD-COMAIRLE BANALTRAN.

(GENERAL NURSING COUNCIL.)

TELEPHONE: 62203.

Please address any reply to—
THE REGISTRAR
and quote No.........................

75 cearnóg muirbtean, o.,
baile áta cliat.
(75 MERRION SQUARE, S.,
DUBLIN.)

Dear Madam,   7th February, 1944.

    I have much pleasure in informing you that you were successful at the recent Examination held by the General Nursing Council.

    When you have completed your three years training please return the attached slip signed by your Matron or Resident Medical Superintendent to this Office for Registration purposes.

                       Yours faithfully,

Miss Adelaide E. Hayes,
Adelaide Hospital,
Dublin.

Annie Black,
R.G.N.
Registrar.

GNC letter, exam results, 1944

Phyllis Noblett,
QAIMNS, on
service WWII

Phyllis Noblett,
QAIMNS, on
service WWII

Hockey team, 1948

Inter-hospital tennis
team, 1948

Left: Children's
party, c. 1940
Right: Children in
Peter St. c. 1950

Left: Sister Crawford
and carol singers,
1948
Right: Sister Douglas
and nurse McKay,
with Santa and
children, Christmas,
c. 1949

Doctor Desmond Bell
and Sister Patricia Bell
(Née Michael), 1956

Nurses Joyce Michael
and Muriel Hammond,
on the roof, c. 1956

Elizabeth Nuzum
with patient, 1947

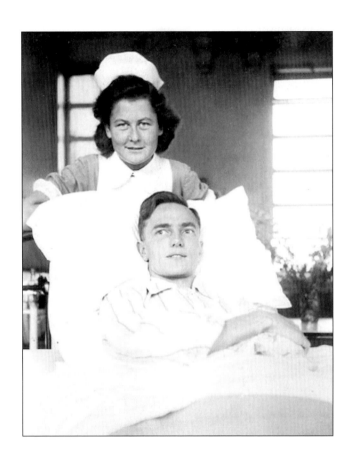

Nurse Selina (Maud)
Fossett on the roof,
c. 1962

Nurses' sitting room, c. 1950

Studying for exams, c 1940

Elizabeth Schweiger
(Née Knaggs),
missionary work,
Bangladesh

Miss Dornan, Matron
and sisters, c. 1962

Noelle Harte (Walker),
1970

Ruvé Steacy,
graduation 1977

Miss Mansfield,
Matron 1980-1990

Prizewinners, 1979-80, *(L to R)* nurses Dukelow, Condell & Patterson

Nurses *(L to R)*
Satchwell, Jones,
Bigley, Benn, Ross,
Ingram, graduation
day 1989

Sarah Condell and
September 1990 set

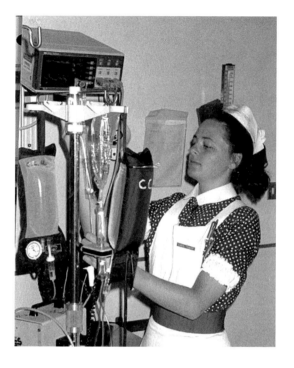

Staff Nurse
Shirley Ingram
in CCU,
c. 1992

L to R Matron Seville,
Avril Shaw & Naomi
Elliott with nurses,
1994

Miss Seville

Miss Seville and staff
fundraising for the
Adelaide, c. 1995

Matron, sisters and nurse tutors, old uniform

Matron, sisters and nurse tutors, new uniform

Nurse Ciara McAssey in
modern AMNCH
uniform

Matron since 1985 and her appointment was widely welcomed by the Adelaide staff. Among her responsibilities on taking office was to continue the work of planning for the move to Tallaght, which included plans for a new amalgamated nursing school. By this time, the Adelaide school was sharing teaching arrangements with the Meath and National Children's hospitals.

As Matron, Yvonne Seville played a key role in planning for the new nursing and nurse training arrangements that would eventually emerge in the new hospital. She was the last head of the Nursing Department at Peter Street and her position was especially strategic, since she was responsible for maintaining and developing the nursing services at Peter Street and also working to ensure the smooth and successful transfer of these same services to Tallaght. In this work she was supported by her deputies and ward sisters, and by Avril Shaw, Principal Tutor, who oversaw the necessary curriculum development work for the changes that were about to take place in nurse training nationally, and which were aimed at giving academic recognition of the nursing qualification through a university diploma.

Miss Seville was also supported by Valerie Houlden, a senior Adelaide nurse, who was appointed the Nurse Planner and later the Commissioner and Planner for the services in the new hospital. Valerie Houlden's role involved working with the numerous user groups across all of the hospitals and services that would eventually move to Tallaght, including psychiatric services at St Loman's Hospital, attending project management meetings with the architects, evaluating new hospital equipment, and helping the hospitals to plan for a common approach to doing things in the future. As a former diabetic nurse specialist, Valerie Houlden knew the importance of gathering all the facts, and she remembers attending one meeting at which engineers expressed their surprise that she had visited the Tallaght site before they had. One particular responsibility she saw was the need to help people to leave the 'comfortable zone' of a 'very nurturing' small hospital, and to move to a larger hospital where, for some, it seemed that an individual's needs might not seem so important in a bigger organisation.

Miss Seville also remembers the challenges in planning for the move to Tallaght and the exhausting work of the three years leading up to the move in 1998; along with managing the Adelaide nursing services, she travelled to Tallaght twice or three times a week to attend numerous meetings, often until 11 o'clock at night. In her annual report to the Nurses' League, she wrote of the 'endless meetings' to which sisters and staff nurses were expected to contribute on 'every aspect of the new hospital, from general layout and policy making to service units and all items of equipment and furnishing.'[36]

With her counterparts in the other hospitals, she was determined to have a successful amalgamation of the three hospitals and she worked at developing good staff relationships for the future. This involved activities like amalgamating sisters' meetings and holding social gatherings together. After 1996, the Adelaide and Meath hospitals interchanged nursing staff across the clinical departments of the two hospitals, as a way of making the transition easier. Miss Seville was aware of the sense of loss and upset that many staff from the three hospitals experienced with the impending closure of their respective hospitals. As a long-serving Adelaide nurse, she too experienced the feeling of loss that accompanied the closure, but in her role as Matron, she felt a strong sense of responsibility to 'keep up my side' as a way of helping others to cope.

Curriculum changes

Of more immediate concern to Miss Seville after she took office was the need to ensure that nursing services were maintained at optimum levels, given that student nurses' availability to work in the service to the hospital was greatly curtailed following the introduction of the new European directives on the training of nurses in 1991. The curriculum changes introduced in that year were aimed at achieving a better balance and better co-ordination between classroom and clinical instruction. In practical terms, each training hospital was required to increase the period of classroom teaching from twenty-eight to forty weeks. This necessitated the recruitment of additional staff nurses for deployment in the clinical departments that were for so long staffed by students. For Miss Seville and the matrons of training hospitals that had relied so heavily on the student workforce, this was a real challenge, which was added to by the need to support qualified nurses in taking postgraduate specialist clinical training, a need which the Adelaide Hospital saw as essential for its ongoing service development.

Miss Seville calculated that the new training regulations meant that there were twenty fewer students available for service at any one time in the Hospital.[37] Aside from the challenge of maintaining nursing service, the expanded curriculum meant that the school was busy all year round with just a few short weeks' break from teaching in the summer period.

At the time, the hospital also needed to recruit additional nurse tutors in order to deliver the additional classroom teaching and meet minimum teacher-student ratios that were also set down in training regulations. The Adelaide was well placed in this regard, since Adelaide nurses Sarah Condell and Naomi Elliott had taken up positions in the school in 1989, having completed the three-year nurse tutor's degree at University College Dublin. This meant that the Adelaide was the first hospital to satisfy the recommended tutor-student ratio of 15:1.[38] At the time, Avril Shaw was the Principal Tutor, and in the early 1990s, nurse tutors Sister Kathleen Russell, Mary Bell and Aoife Russell joined the school, and the school's day-to-day administration was supported by Mrs Irvine and Miss O'Neill.

In the final years at Peter Street, the school was training approximately thirty-four students annually. In 1989, eleven additional students who had commenced their training at Dr Steevens' Hospital were admitted to the Adelaide School to complete their training when Dr Steevens' closed. This marked a significant event in the history of the Adelaide School, since Roman Catholics were admitted to the school for the first time. Another milestone was the recruitment of the first male students, Mark Pierce and Daniel Nuzum, in autumn 1991. Mark Pierce had been a former teacher and after qualifying as a nurse, he travelled abroad to work in nursing in London. Daniel Nuzum married fellow Adelaide nurse Heather Whiteside, and later became a clergyman, and at the time of writing, was Hospital Chaplain at University College Hospital Cork.

The new training regulations introduced in 1991 were asserting the principle that due regard had to be given to the content and the quality of student learning. While the hospitals continued to recruit and employ students, the major effect of the new regulations was to remove much of the hospitals' control over the conduct of nurse training.[39] In the Adelaide, practical expressions of this change in emphasis included the wearing of mufti in class, tutors addressing students by their first name in class, and the shift of responsibility for administering student clinical allocations from Matron's Office to the nursing school.[40] The change also impacted on ward staff, who had to adjust to the fact that students were being seen less and less as service employees. In 1995 Avril Brady (nee Shaw) was appointed as a lecturer in the Royal College of Surgeons in Ireland and her colleague Joan FitzPatrick became the last Principal Tutor at the Adelaide School in Peter Street.

Diploma in Nursing

At a national level, two significant events concerning nurse training took place in 1994. In that year, the Nursing Board published a report entitled *The Future of Nurse Education and Training in Ireland*.[41] The report pointed to the inherent difficulty of the student nurse's dual role as worker and learner, and it recommended the establishment of links with higher education in order to afford full student status to nurses in training. Also in that year, a diploma in nursing course was instituted at University College Galway, involving a three-year university diploma course in which students were recruited and employed in the health services and also had the status of registered university students. The so-called 'Galway Model' was presented as a pilot course, but resistance from nursing unions to a possible two-tier preparatory training system developing, the poor value for money that the training system had come to represent, and a momentum for change resulted in a government decision to roll out the diploma model on a national basis in all the nurse training schools.

The Adelaide Board welcomed the advent of university recognition for nurse training, and in 1995 it established a special committee to plan for the new three-year university diploma, and work commenced on the necessary curriculum planning and staff preparation. The advent of the diploma in effect meant that the earlier planning for a degree in nursing with Trinity College was redundant. The government approved funding for the course to commence in 1996 in partnership with the School of Nursing and Midwifery at Trinity College Dublin. The school at Trinity was founded in 1996 to enable the development of undergraduate and post-graduate courses in the Faculty of Health Sciences.[42]

The first group of 39 Adelaide nursing students entered the new diploma course in 1996, marking the ending of the system of apprenticeship training that had been in place at the Adelaide for almost 150 years. The new course had many of the characteristics of traditional training, with a strong emphasis on clinical training. Students of the three constituent hospitals that would soon form the new Tallaght Hospital were now attending lectures together at the Trinity College campus. Lecture theatres were also used at the nearby Royal College of Surgeons in Ireland.

For the Adelaide, the most profound change brought about by the new diploma course was the altered status of student nurses, who were now nursing students, and who for most of the training period would not have responsibility for providing nursing service in the hospital. New supports for the clinical training element of the course were introduced at the time; these included a Nurse Practice Development Co-ordinator and clinical placement co-ordinators to support and assist students while on clinical placement.

Move to Tallaght
Underpinned by the legal arrangements of the Tallaght Hospital Charter of 1996, the future place of the Adelaide Nursing School was assured. The most outward public symbol of the Adelaide School was its nurses' uniform and

the essential 'traditional characteristics' of the uniform would also be retained in the new Tallaght Hospital uniform. The Adelaide Hospital Society became the body responsible for selecting the nursing students for the new diploma in nursing course.

In 1996 the Adelaide School produced a promotional video and promoted nurse training at the Adelaide School among secondary schools. In that same year, the Adelaide Hospital Society established a Nursing Development Fund to provide annual bursaries, grants and scholarships to nursing students. The Fund was aimed at a range of activities from undergraduate and postgraduate education to research, and one objective was to ensure that no applicant to the Adelaide School would be precluded from training due to financial reasons. In addition, the Society envisaged providing enhanced opportunities for staff nurses to undertake continuing professional training and awarding fellowships to nurse tutors to pursue master and doctoral programmes of study. In its first year, €57,000 was raised for the Fund from a range of fundraising activities, including nurses' tea parties, charity walks and raffles.

In the period of transition, the Adelaide Board took a decision to admit non-Protestant students, and while the decision was somewhat pragmatic, being based on reduced numbers applying at the time, it reflected the Adelaide ethos of inclusiveness. The retention of selection interviews under the auspices of the Adelaide Hospital Society following the introduction of a national centralised system of recruitment to nursing in 2002 maintained the Society's prerogative in ensuring the participation of the Protestant community in healthcare through nurse training.

Amalgamated College of Nursing and Centre for Nurse Education
The terms of the Adelaide Hospital Charter provided for the establishment of a new College of Nursing, which would retain 'the great traditions' of the nursing schools of the Adelaide, Meath and National Children's hospitals, and it included 'a solemn agreement' to retain forty places each year for 'suitably qualified Protestant student nurses.'[43] With the move to Tallaght complete in 1998, the College of Nursing was established in June of that year. Comprising the three distinct nursing schools, the college was a constituent part of the Faculty of Health Sciences of Trinity College Dublin, and was located in the new Education Centre at Tallaght Hospital.

The new Tallaght Hospital opened to patients on 21 June 1998. Its first Director of Nursing was Mary McCarthy, the former Director of Nursing at the Meath Hospital, and the first Principal Tutor of the Amalgamated College of Nursing was Sarah Condell, then a nurse tutor at the Adelaide

School. The 'dear old Adelaide' on Peter Street was sold in that same year. Many Adelaide staff remembered that the final push to move services to Tallaght seemed to happen rather quickly. For the new hospital authorities, the joy of opening was tempered by a failure on the part of the government to make good its commitment to fully fund the services that had been transferred to the new hospital. The Chief Executive Officer David McCuthceon saw this as a breach of trust and resigned.[44]

In the six month period before the move to Tallaght, Sarah Condell occupied the Principal Tutor's office in the Meath Hospital and made regular visits to the new teaching facilities in Tallaght to ensure all was in readiness for the move. Despite the detailed planning for the move, when it eventually happened, Sarah Condell also remembers the sense of the suddenness of being 'shipped out' when the movers arrived.

With its distinct identity in the new Amalgamated College of Nursing and located in new modern teaching facilities at Tallaght, the Adelaide Hospital School of Nursing continued its core business of nurse training, now in partnership with Trinity College Dublin School of Nursing and Midwifery. In the period after 1998 the College of Nursing was responsible for delivering the new nursing diploma course. The course comprised a general nursing diploma and psychiatric nursing diploma to cater for the psychiatric services of St Loman's Hospital, which were also incorporated into the Tallaght Hospital.

The first five years of the College of Nursing at Tallaght were marked by further change. Aside from the work of establishing the new amalgamated College as an integral part of a new hospital and delivering a new diploma course, the college was already planning for further major changes that would come with the introduction of a new degree in nursing in 2002. Through this work, the partnership with Trinity College Dublin was being developed and consolidated, and would further strengthen the position of the new Tallaght Hospital as a constituent hospital of the Trinity College Faculty of Health Sciences.

Degree in Nursing
Related to dissatisfaction with conditions of employment, industrial unrest among nurses in the mid 1990s led the government to establish a Commission on Nursing, which had a remit to undertake a broad examination of nursing in Ireland, including the educational preparation of nurses.[45] The Commission published its Report entitled *A Blueprint for the Future* in 1998, and among its most far-reaching proposals was the recommendation to

replace the recently introduced diploma in nursing course with a four-year honours degree as the route to professional preparation and registration for nurses. The diploma model was held to have failed to give nurses in training the full benefits of a third-level education, and the training offered by an honours degree was held to be more in keeping with the professional training needs of nurses for the future.

The government accepted the recommendations in the Commission's Report and gave a commitment to fund the complete transfer of preparatory training into the universities and institutes of technology in 2002. The financial arrangements provided for the building of new nursing schools on university campuses and the transfer of suitably qualified teaching staff who were then working in the hospital nursing schools. At the time, many of the tutors in the College of Nursing at Tallaght transferred to the School of Nursing and Midwifery at Trinity College Dublin to take up positions as college lecturers. This group included Naomi Elliott, the only Adelaide School nurse tutor to do so.

Planning

In the time leading up to the introduction of the new degree course, the Adelaide Hospital Society entered into discussions with Trinity College, the Nursing Board and the Central Applications Office to agree the procedures that would permit the Society to 'facilitate its national responsibilities to nominate … students each year to the Adelaide School'.[46] Dr David Moore represented the Society on the Nursing Education Forum, the national body established to set out the principles for developing and delivering the new degree programme. The careful planning for the introduction of the degree bore fruit, and in October 2002, the first cohort of undergraduate nursing students, including thirty five Adelaide School students recruited by the Society, entered the new course at Trinity. In that year the Society awarded the Adelaide Nursing Scholarship and a number of bursaries. In 2003, well in excess of eight hundred individuals made an application to the Adelaide School of Nursing for the thirty-five places available.

With the introduction of the nursing degree in 2002, the role and status of the College of Nursing at Tallaght changed. The advent of the degree in nursing meant the full integration of nursing students into Trinity College Dublin, and the College of Nursing no longer admitted nursing students undergoing undergraduate preparatory training. Accordingly, its role changed and its new remit was to conduct continuing professional education and in-service training, and to provide and support postgraduate clinical training for nurses in association with Trinity College. With this change of role, the college was re-designated the Regional Centre of Nurse Education for the Health Service Executive (HSE), Dublin and Mid-Leinster. The centre became one of a number of regional centres of nurse education that were established after 2002 when hospital nursing schools were no longer responsible for preparatory nurse training. Jim Walsh, former Principal Tutor at the Health Service Executive, was appointed the Director of the centre, and the centre became responsible for in-service training and continuing professional development for nurses from across a large region of south-west Dublin, Kildare and Wicklow.

The Adelaide Hospital Society continues to manage the Adelaide School and each year it awards the Eileen Mansfield Scholarship and Student Nurse Bursary, and the Dorothy and David Mitchell Scholarship. Winners of the Eileen Mansfield Scholarship in the early years included Steve Pittman, Mary Wynne, Shirley Ingram, Joan Love, and Mary Noonan. In 2006, almost 150 years after the founding of the Adelaide School, the first nursing students from the Adelaide School of Nursing graduated with nursing degrees from Trinity College Dublin, and the tradition of nurse training at the Adelaide School entered a new era.

CHAPTER EIGHT

'Assiduous and intelligent nursing': The Adelaide School and the Adelaide Nurse

'I'm so glad and proud to be an Adelaide-trained nurse
and [I] wear the badge with pride.'[1]

Established in 1859 as a training school for young Protestant women, the Adelaide Hospital School of Nursing in Dublin was the first nurse training school for lay women in Ireland. The school was a key part of an institution founded to give 'medical attendance, and also pastoral support and consolation, exclusively to Protestants in reduced circumstances', and this 'peculiar religious character' of the Adelaide Hospital remained a fundamental part of its constitution, giving clear direction to its management policies and to its approaches to treatment and care.

The Adelaide School

Religious tensions were an abiding feature of public life in Ireland in the nineteenth century and were played out in public disputes surrounding the Adelaide Hospital's constitution and role as a distinctly Protestant institution in a city where Catholic nationalism was emerging and growing in confidence. In the face of such disputes the Adelaide School provided professionally-trained nurses who proffered 'assiduous and intelligent nursing' to the people of Dublin and to the whole of Ireland. The school developed a national reputation as a place for training nurses who excelled in their standards of nursing. With her distinctive uniform of blue cotton with white hail spot, the Adelaide nurse was readily identifiable as she went about her nursing duties in the hospital or in private nursing.

The early decades for the new Adelaide School were characterised by mixed fortunes, with periods when it seemed that the training of probationers was barely happening, to years of great progress, brought about by the efforts of matrons like Sarah Ruttle and Lucinda Sullivan. The early decades were also characterised by severe financial difficulties that at times threatened the future of the hospital and its school.

The success of the Adelaide as a modern hospital at the forefront of scientific medicine was in great part attributable to the skilled nursing care that was proffered under the system of modern nursing that had been introduced

in the nineteenth century. At the turn of the twentieth century, the Adelaide
School was established as one of Dublin's most prominent training schools.
It was managed by a committee of medical men and laymen who took major
policy decisions concerning the training of nurses, although the day-to-day
management of the hospital and its training arrangements were in the hands
of capable and progressive women like Henrietta Poole, Gertrude Knight,
and Henrietta Hill, and later Margaret Dornan, Eileen Mansfield, Yvonne
Seville and the school's many nurse tutors.

The Great War placed many additional demands on Adelaide nurses, and
many gave service as military nurses in the war. The attainment of women's
suffrage and state registration of nursing were important achievements for
nursing in the period after the 1914-18 war. The difficult economic circumstances of the inter-war period in Ireland and the privations of the
Emergency provided the context for the experiences of the hospital and its
Nursing School. In this period, the Adelaide probationer experienced a
regime that demanded obedience, loyalty and the strict observance of rules.

In the decades after 1950, the Adelaide Hospital continued to expand its
services, and through a policy of modernisation to meet the needs of patients
and staff, the hospital continued to play a key role in the provision of modern hospital services in Dublin. Medical technology and hospital modernisation greatly increased the capital and running costs of the hospital, and in
1960 the Adelaide took the extreme measure of accepting state funding to
meet its day-to-day costs.

While the hospital remained as an independent institution in the period,
its place as one of a number of medium-sized hospitals in Dublin meant that
it featured in government plans to develop larger but fewer hospitals. After a
protracted period of uncertainty about the future of the Adelaide Hospital
and its particular denominational ethos, the Tallaght Hospital Charter of
1996 provided the mechanism for the retention of the Adelaide's 'unique
position as the focus for minority participation in health care' and established the new Tallaght Hospital as a focus for continuing Protestant participation in the health services.

The training of nurses at the Adelaide School was an important expression of the hospital's distinct character, and the Adelaide tradition found
particular expression in its seemingly traditional, yet paradoxically, progressive training school. The school played a significant role in preserving the
Adelaide tradition throughout the twentieth century and became an important vehicle for carrying that tradition into the 'new Ireland', when the
Adelaide Hospital finally closed and was amalgamated with the Meath and

National Children's Hospitals to form the new Tallaght Hospital Dublin in 1998.

The Adelaide nurse

The Adelaide Hospital led the way in introducing modern systems of nursing and nurse training in the nineteenth century, and throughout the twentieth century, the hospital's nursing department remained at the heart of developments in professional practice and education, both within and beyond the Adelaide. While its matrons and other senior nurses feature most prominently in the archives of the Adelaide Hospital, its nurse tutors and staff nurses were part of the cadre of progressive nurses that brought the Adelaide ideals of service and skilled nursing with them when they travelled abroad. Adelaide nurses were always open to outside ideas and influences as they conducted their nursing and teaching. While the Adelaide was a relatively small hospital, its nurses were and remain at the forefront of developments in clinical practice, education, research, and professional policy. Many Adelaide nurses who trained in the last decades at Peter Street, like Sarah Condell, Naomi Elliott and Shirley Ingram, typify the new cadre of modern Adelaide nurse.

Naomi Elliott commenced training in 1975 and was the gold medallist in her set. After qualifying, she studied midwifery in Aberdeen and afterwards studied intensive care nursing at the Royal Infirmary in Edinburgh. Following a period as an intensive care staff nurse in Edinburgh and later as a cardio-thoracic nurse in New Zealand, she returned to the Adelaide in 1984, bringing new skills and new ideas to her work in the hospital's intensive care unit. Sarah Condell commenced training in 1978, and was top of her class in her final examinations. She studied midwifery in Glasgow and returned to the Adelaide after three years as a midwife in Scotland. On her return to the Adelaide, she worked in a variety of medical and surgical settings, and in 1986, she and Naomi Elliott were asked by Miss Mansfield to undertake the three-year nurse tutor degree course at University College Dublin.

At a time of great change in nurse training in Ireland, both Sarah Condell and Naomi Elliott returned to the Adelaide as nursing graduates and registered tutors, after which time they worked with Avril Brady and other colleagues on the important curriculum planning and staff development work in preparation for the introduction of the nursing diploma in 1996. Sarah Condell was the first Principal Tutor of the new Amalgamated College of Nursing at Tallaght and with her colleagues at the Adelaide, Meath and National Children's nursing schools, facilitated the successful transfer of nurse training from the three city centre hospitals to Tallaght.

Today Sarah Condell holds a joint appointment of Nursing Research Advisor at the Health Research Board and Research Development Officer with the National Council for the Professional Development of Nursing and Midwifery (NCNM), the body responsible for developing and approving professional clinical roles. In these joint roles she is a leader of nursing and midwifery research policy and of practice development in Ireland. She holds an MA degree, and at the time of writing, was completing a PhD at Trinity College Dublin. Naomi Elliott completed a master's degree at Queen's University Belfast, and for two years acted as an Education Officer at the Nursing Board. Following the introduction of the preparatory degree in nursing in 2002, she was appointed a lecturer at Trinity College Dublin and afterwards completed a PhD, also at Queen's.

Shirley Ingram entered training in 1985 and her first black belt position in the coronary care unit (CCU) introduced her to cardiology nursing, which has remained the focus of her clinical work to the present day. The small four-bedded CCU at the Adelaide cared for acutely ill patients and gave her the rich clinical experience that stood her in good stead as she took responsibility for night time front-line emergency care throughout the hospital. She later gained valuable clinical experience in Australia and on her return in 1993, completed a course in Coronary Care Nursing at Beaumont Hospital, and then returned to the Adelaide.

In 1994, she began working in the fledgling Adelaide and Meath cardiac rehabilitation service with Joan Love, and both she and Joan were among the first nurses in Ireland to achieve the grade of Clinical Nurse Specialist. Over the next twelve years, she worked to develop cardiac rehabilitation services and oversee their successful transfer to Tallaght. A founding member of the committee that instituted the Master of Science (MSc) in Cardiac Rehabilitation with Trinity College in 2002, she herself completed an MSc degree by research in 2003. She served for many years on the Committee of the Irish Association of Cardiac Rehabilitation (IACR), and served as IACR President from 2004 to 2006. Since 2007, Shirley Ingram has acted in the role of Clinical Nurse Manager in Cardiology Nursing at Tallaght, bringing her extensive education, research and service development expertise to the running a large clinical department comprising diagnostic, treatment and rehabilitation services and a nine-bedded coronary care unit. She is a past recipient of the Eileen Mansfield Scholarship. In 2008, Shirley Ingram was elected a governor of the Adelaide Hospital Society.

Sarah Condell, Naomi Elliott and Shirley Ingram are among many Adelaide nurses who are leaders in their respective areas in nursing. Their work represents the spectrum of modern nursing, encompassing expert clinical practice, service management, teaching, research, professional policy, and practice development. In their respective roles, they each carry the Adelaide tradition of 'assiduous and intelligent nursing' in the twenty-first century.

The Adelaide Hospital Society in the 21st Century

Today the Adelaide Hospital Society continues to support and maintain the Adelaide, Meath and National Children's Hospital as 'a public voluntary teaching hospital consistent with the Christian ethos and medical ethics of the Protestant community.' Consistent with the provisions of the Tallaght Hospital Charter, the Society retains responsibility for selecting students for the new nursing degree programme at Trinity College Dublin. This responsibility remains unique to the Adelaide Hospital Society. As a voluntary charitable and Christian organisation, the Society retained 'a peculiar regard for the historic involvement of the Protestant churches through lay voluntary commitment to hospital care', and at the same time, it embraced the changes that were occurring in nursing education in the wake of the Report of the Commission on Nursing in 1998.[2]

After its reconstitution as a charitable company, the Adelaide Hospital Society continued to play a central role in the life of the new Tallaght Hospital, and today it also plays an important role in wider public life as a contributor to public debates on matters of national importance within the field of healthcare, social policy, and other matters of public concern. In its first year as a newly consolidated Society it prepared and published a detailed and influential submission to the Forum for Peace and Reconciliation, the only hospital to do so, and it also made an oral presentation to the Forum. It also made a submission to the Commission on Assisted Human Reproduction and submissions on legislation on voluntary activity, and it published important position papers on a range of social issues, including active citizenship, inequities and inequalities in access to health care, social health insurance, and models for the future funding of health services in Ireland.[3] The Society's various submissions and position papers have made an important contribution to public life for the good of Irish society. The Society continues to contribute to national debates through the publication of position papers and by participating in debates in national news media.

The Adelaide Hospital Society's proactive stance in addressing real and challenging social issues that confront Ireland in the early twenty-first century demonstrates considerable courage. It also demonstrates the Adelaide Hospital's legacy of voluntary participation, and its value of caring for the weaker members of society. The Society's role in embracing the many changes in nurse training in the years leading up to 2002 and ensuring the successful continuation of the Adelaide School in the twenty-first century is consistent with the Adelaide tradition of being outward looking and progressive while retaining the values held by the founders, supporters and staff of the Adelaide Hospital Dublin down through more than 150 years.[4]

End Notes

CHAPTER ONE

1. M, E. Daly, 'Late nineteenth and early twentieth century Dublin', In: Harkness D and O'Dowd M (eds) *Historical Studies xi. The town in Ireland*, Belfast: Appletree Press, 1981, pp. 221–52.

2. Cited in P. Gatenby, *Dublin's Meath Hospital*, Dublin: Town House, 1996, p. 4.

3. Cited in T. Farmar, *Patients, Potions and Physicians: a Social History of Medicine in Ireland*, Dublin: A&A Farmar, 2004, p. 64.

4. J. Prunty, *Managing the Dublin Slums, 1850–1922*, Dublin: Dublin City Press Libraries, 2004.

5. G. M. Fealy, *A History of Apprenticeship Nurse Training in Ireland*, London: Routledge, 2006, pp. 17-20. In this period, the city's two large Catholic hospitals, St Vincent's Hospital at St Stephen's Green (1834) and the Mater Misericordiae Hospital on Eccles Street (1861) were also founded.

6. Historians David Mitchell and Fergus O'Ferrall have provided authoritative accounts of the history of the Adelaide Hospital Dublin, and their accounts have included analysis of the motivations of the Hospital's original founders in the mid-nineteenth century, as well as details of the work and efforts of their successors as guardians of the 'fundamental principle', upon which the Hospital was founded. See D. Mitchell, *A Peculiar Place: The Adelaide Hospital Dublin 1839-1979*, Dublin: Blackwater, 1989; F. O'Ferrall, *The Adelaide Hospital, Dublin, 1839-2008*, Dublin: The Adelaide Hospital Society, 2008.

7. Adelaide Hospital Dublin (Hereafter AHD) Inaugural Address delivered in the Theatre of the Adelaide Hospital Peter Street at the Commencement of the Clinical Session, 2 November 1858, Dublin: George Herbert, p. 11.

8. O'Ferrall, *The Adelaide Hospital*, p. 4.

9. Cited at The National Trust (1982; repr. 1994) *Sudbury Hall*, pp. 29-30, Available online at: http://en.wikipedia.org/wiki/Adelaide_of_Saxe-Meiningen#cite_note-28 (Accessed 10 September 2008).

10. Cited in Mitchell, *Peculiar Place*, pp. 34-35

11. Ibid., p. 39.

12. Cited in annual reports of the Adelaide Hospital Dublin.

13. House of Commons, *Report of the Select Committee on Dublin Hospitals, Minutes of Evidence, Appendix and Index*, H.C. Dublin: HMSO, 1854 (383), p. 217 (Evidence of Dr Dominic Corrigan).

14. AHD, *The First Annual Report of the Adelaide Hospital*, 1859, pp. 10 and 15.

15. Ibid., p. 15.

16. Duncan, Inaugural Address, 1858.

17. AHD, *The Eleventh Annual Report of the Adelaide Hospital for the Year ending 31st December 1868*, Dublin: Adelaide Hospital, 1869, pp. 11-12.

18. Select Committee on Dublin Hospitals, June 29, 1854, (Evidence of Dr Thomas Brady), p. 100.

19. Duncan, Inaugural Address, p. 5.

20. Ibid., pp 18-19.

21. AHD, Introductory lecture delivered in the Adelaide Hospital, Dublin at the Commencement of the Clinical Course 31 October 1864, Dublin: Adelaide Hospital.
22. Cited in J. Robins, *The Miasma: Epidemic and Panic in Nineteenth-century Ireland,* Dublin: Institute of Public Administration, 1995.
23. AHD, Fundamental Principle. Office of the Adelaide Hospital October 1858, p. 32.
24. AHD, First Annual Report of the Adelaide Hospital, Dublin: Adelaide Hospital, 1859, pp. 14-15.
25. O'Ferrall, *Adelaide Hospital,* p. 14.
26. AHD, The Second Annual Report of the Adelaide Hospital for the Year ending 31st December 1859, Dublin: Adelaide Hospital, 1860, p. 11.
27. AHD, The Third Annual Report of the Adelaide Hospital for the Year ending 31st December 1860, 1859, Dublin: Adelaide Hospital, 1861, p. 17.
28. AHD, The Eight Annual Report of the Adelaide Hospital for the Year ending 31st December 1865, Dublin: Adelaide Hospital, 1866, p. 11.
29. AHD, The Fourth Annual Report of the Adelaide Hospital for the Year ending 31st December 1861, Dublin: Adelaide Hospital, 1862, p. 14.
30. Adelaide Hospital Dublin/Manuscript/Managing Committee/(hereafter AHD/MS/MC) /11270/64/1863–67, 28 December 1866.
31. Ibid.
32. AHD, The Tenth Annual Report of the Adelaide Hospital for the Year ending 31st December 1867, Dublin: Adelaide Hospital, 1868, p. 14.
33. Ibid, p. 17.
34. Ibid. p. 18.
35. AHD, The Thirteenth Annual Report of the Adelaide Hospital for the Year ending 31st December 1870, 1871, Dublin: Adelaide Hospital, pp. 11-12.
36. AHD, The Fourteenth Annual Report of the Adelaide Hospital for the Year ending 31st December 1871, Dublin: Adelaide Hospital, 1872, p. 11.
37. AHD, The Fifteenth Annual Report of the Adelaide Hospital for the Year ending 31st December 1872, Dublin: Adelaide Hospital, 1873, pp. 11-12.
38. G. Fealy & J. Harford, 'Nervous energy and administrative ability': The early lady principals and lady superintendents in Ireland.' *Journal of Educational Administration & History* 39 (3), 2007, 271-283.
39. AHD, The Sixteenth Annual Report of the Adelaide Hospital for the Year ending 31st December 1873, Dublin: Adelaide Hospital, 1874, p. 11.
40. Ibid., p. 13.
41. I am grateful to Anthony Giles, Sunbeam House Trust, for his great generosity in providing biographical and other valuable primary and secondary source materials on Lucinda Sullivan, and for his helpful suggestions on the narrative.
42. L. Sullivan, *Mrs Lucinda Sullivan Diary of a Month in Mannedorf, with an account of the loss of the "St. Gotthard" on the Lake of Zurich,* Dublin, 1873.
43. L. Sullivan, *An Address delivered at a meeting held in Dublin on 15th October 1879,* Dublin: Young Women's Christian Association 1879, p. 6 (original emphasis).
44. M. Luddy, 'Women and charity work in nineteenth-century Ireland: The historical background': In Loughrey F,. *Sunbeam House Bray,* Dublin: The Trustees: Sunbeam House, pp. iv–xix.
45. Ibid., p. xviii.
46. Loughrey, *Sunbeam House,* p. 17.
47. AHD, The Eighteenth Annual Report of the Adelaide Hospital for the Year ending 31st December 1875, Dublin: Adelaide Hospital, 1876, p. 12.
48. AHD, The Twentieth Annual Report of the Adelaide Hospital for the Year ending 31st

December 1877, Dublin: Adelaide Hospital, 1878, p. 12.

CHAPTER TWO

1. Dublin Evening Mail, 5 December 1877, Insert in Manuscript Adelaide Hospital Dublin Managing Committee (hereafter MS/AHD/MC)/11270/62.
2. Ibid.
3. Fealy, *Apprenticeship Training*, 2006, p. 17; A. Wickham 'A better scheme for nursing: the influence of the Dublin Hospital Sunday Fund on nursing and nurse training in Ireland in the nineteenth century', *International History of Nursing Journal* 6 (2), 2001, pp. 26-35.
4. A. Bradshaw, *The Nurse Apprentice, 1860–1977*, Aldershot: Ashgate, p. 3.
5. Fealy & Harford, 'Nervous energy', 2007, p. 273.
6. Fealy, *Apprenticeship Training*, pp. 19-20.
7. Ibid., p. G. Fealy, *A History of the Provision and Reform of General Nurse Education and Training in Ireland, 1879–1994*, PhD. dissertation, University College Dublin, 2002, Chapter 4.
8. MS Board of Governors Proceedings, Sir Patrick Dun's Hospital, 10 December, *1878*, p. 54.
9. O'Ferrall, *The Adelaide Hospital*, p. 14.
10. J. McKinlay Calder, *The Story of Nursing*, London: Methuen, 1971, p. 48.
11. T. P. C. Kirkpatrick, *The History of Dr. Steevens' Hospital 1720-1920*, Dublin: University Press, 1924, p. 281-282.
12. Fealy, *Apprenticeship Training*, pp. 27-31.
13. Ibid., pp. 21-26. At its founding in 1874, it was anticipated that the Fund would be a national movement in which both Protestant and Catholic churches would participate. However, the Roman Catholic Hierarchy in Dublin failed to back the movement, and hence the Catholic hospitals did not benefit from monies raised by the Fund.
14. Ibid. For a detailed discussion of the position of the Catholic Church at the time, see A. Wickham 'A better scheme for nursing', 2000.
15. Dublin Hospital Sunday Fund (Hereafter DHSF), *Annual Report for the Year 1878*, 1879, Dublin: Browne and Nolan, p. 11; Fealy, *Apprenticeship Training*, 2006, pp. 19-27.
16. The Committee on Nursing had a membership of eleven. The Committee visited Sir Patrick Dun's, the City of Dublin, Dr Steevens, the Meath, Mercer's, Whitworth (Drumcondra), the Coombe Lying-in, the Rotunda Lying-in, St Mark's Ophthalmic, the National Eye and Ear Infirmary, Cork Street Fever Hospital, Rathdown, the Dublin Orthopaedic, and the Adelaide. Dr Lombe Athill of the Adelaide became a member of the Committee in 1879.
17. DHSF, *Report of the Council for the Year 1879* (containing *Report on the Nursing Arrangements in the Hospitals receiving Aid from the Dublin Hospitals Sunday Fund*), Dublin: Browne and Nolan, 1879.
18. Ibid.
19. DHSF, *Annual Report for the Year 1878*, 1879, p. 11.
20. Ibid., p. 15.
21. Fealy, *Apprenticeship Training*, p. 28; See also Wickham, 'A better scheme for nursing', passim.
22. DHSF, *Annual Report for the Year 1879*, 1880, p. 13.
23. Ibid, p. 34.
24. Ibid., 12 November 1878
25. Cited in Mitchell, *A Peculiar Place*, p. 88.
26. DHSF, *Annual Report for the Year 1879*, 1880, pp. 35-36.
27. MS/AHD/MC/11270/62, 22 January 1880.
28. AHD, *Twenty-third Annual Meeting of the Governors and Members of the Adelaide*

Hospital, 29 March *1881*; Wickham, 'A better scheme for nursing', 2000, p. 14.

29. St Patrick's Home was located at 101 St Stephen's Green.

30. Ibid., 10 May 1881.

31. MS/AHD/MC/11270/62, 15 June 1880.

32. Fealy, *Apprenticeship Training*, 2006, p. 62.

33. MS/AHD/MC/11270/62, 23 November 1880.

34. AHD *Twenty-third Annual Report for the Year ending 31st December 1880,* Dublin: AHD, 1881, p. 10.

35. AHD *Twentieth Annual Report for the year ending 1877,* Dublin: AHD, 1878; AHD *Twenty-first Annual Report for the year ending 1878*, Dublin: AHD, 1879.

36. MSAHD/MC/11260/62, 26 June 1879.

37. AHD *Twenty-second Annual Report for the year ending 1879*, Dublin: AHD, 1880.

38. AHD *Twentieth Annual Report for the year ending 1877*, Dublin: AHD, 1878.

39. MSAHD/MC/11260/62, 20 February 1880.

40. Ibid., April 1880.

41. Ibid., 25 May, 1880.

42. Ibid., 1 June 1880.

43. AHD *Twenty-third Annual Report for the year ending 1880*, Dublin: AHD, 1881.

44. In April 1883, Mr S. F. Adair, a member of the Adelaide Hospital Managing Committee, was nominated to the Council of the Dublin Hospital Sunday Fund.

45. The Ledwich Medical School closed in 1889 when it was became part of the Royal College of Surgeons in Ireland.

46. AHD *Twenty-ninth Annual Report of the Adelaide Hospital for the Year ending 31st December 1886,* Dublin: AHD, 1887, p. 11.

CHAPTER THREE

1. MS/AHD/MC/11270/62, 17 April 1888.

2. Ibid., 12 June 1888.

3. MS/AHD/Nursing Committee (hereafter NC)/11270/58, 1888-1902, 8 October 1888.

4. Ibid.

5. Ibid.

6. Ibid., 17 October 1888 and 31 October 1988.

7. Ibid., 11 December 1888; SG *The Nursing Record* (hereafter NR), 2 (47), 21 February 1889, p. 124.

8. Anon., NR, 15 November 1888, p. 464.

9. Anon., NR, 10 April 1890, p. 180.

10. Anon., NR, 7 November 1888.

11. Anon., NR, 14 November 1888.

12. SG, 'Nursing Echoes', *NR*, 105 (4), 3 April 1890, pp. 164-5.

13. Ibid., p. 165.

14. Ibid.

15. S. McGann 'The development of nursing as an accountable profession', In: Tilley S. and Watson R., *Accountability in Nursing and Midwifery*, Oxford: Blackwell Publishing, pp. 2-20.

16. Anon., BJN, 10 July, 1897, p. 23.

17. H. Poole, 'The registration of asylum attendants as nurses' *NR*, 18, 23 January 1897, p 83.

18. Anon., *The British Journal of Nursing* (hereafter *BJN*), 16 March 1907, p. 197.

19. Anon., *BJN*, 2 March 1895, p. 133. Original emphasis.

20. Anon., 1910 'The passing bell', *BJN*, 45, 1910, p. 9.

21. Anon., *The Nursing Record & Hospital World*, 12 March 1898, p 211.

22. MS/AHD/MC/11270/61, 1895-1906, 13 October 1896.

23. Ibid.

24. Anon., 'The nurses of the Irish Hospitals, No. III. – Adelaide Hospital Nursing School', *The Lady of the House* (hereafter *LoH*), January 15, 1895 15, p. 7.

25. For a discussion on the system of dual probationership, see J. Brooks, 'Structured by class, bound by gender', *International History of Nursing Journal*, 6 (2), 2001, pp. 13-21.

26. Anon. 'Adelaide Hospital Nursing School', 1895, p. 7.

27. MS/AHD/MC/11270/58, 1888–1902, 8 February 1892.

28. Anon. 'Adelaide Hospital Nursing School', 1895, p. 7.

29. Oral testimony VH, 2008.

30. Anon., 'Adelaide Hospital Nursing School', 1895, p. 7.

31. League of Adelaide Hospital Nurses *Bulletin*, Dublin: League of Adelaide Nurses, 1946, p. 4.

32. MS/AHD/MC/11270/58, 1888-1902, 6 March, 1895.

33. MS/AHD/MC/11270/61, 1895-1906, 18 February, 1896.

34. Ibid., 21 February 2005.

35. Fealy, *Apprenticeship Training*, pp 77-79. For academic discussions of the role and symbolism of nurses' uniforms, see A. Pearson, H. Baker, K. Walsh and M. Fitzgerald, 'Contemporary nurses' uniforms: History and traditions', *Journal of Nursing Management*, 9, 2001, pp. 147-152 and J A Barber, 'Uniform and nursing reform', *International History of Nursing Journal*, 3 (1), 1998, pp. 20-29.

36. Anon. 'Adelaide Hospital Nursing School', *LoH*, 15 January, 1895, p. 7.

37. Oral testimony of Judith Chavasse, 1998.

38. Ibid.

39. MS/AHD/NC/11270/58, 8 July 1889.

40. Anon., 'The nurses of the Irish Hospitals, No. VI – The Lady Nurses of the Red Cross Order', *The Lady of the House*, 15 April, 1895, p. 5. The Red Cross lady nurses attended the Meath Hospital and the National Children's Hospital, for clinical instruction. See also Fealy, *Apprenticeship Training*, Chapter 4.

41. Anon., *NR*, 22 August 1889, 73 (3), pp. 121-122.

42. Anon., 'Adelaide Hospital Nursing School', 1895, p. 5.

43. MS/AHD/NC/11270/58, 8 April 1889.

44. Anon., *NR*, 1 June 1893, pp. 271-3.

45. Anon., *NR*, 20 June 1896, Suppl.

CHAPTER FOUR

1. Anon., *The Nursing Record* 18, 16 Jan 1897, p. 58.

2. Y. McEwen, *It's a Long Way to Tipperary: British and Irish Nurses in the Great War*, Dunfermline: Cualann Press, pp. 18-19.

3. MS/AHD/MC/11270/61, 1895–1906, 21 February 1899.

4. Ibid., 20 May 1901.

5. Ibid., 24 January 1899.

6. Ibid., 28 May 1901 (insert).

7. Ibid., 16 December 1902.

8. Anon., *BJN* 59, 20 December 1902, p. 511.

9. MS/AHD/MC/11270/61, 1895-1906, 12 June 1900.

10. AHF/MS/MC/11270/63 Nurses' Biography 1877–1919.

11. M. J. Fitzgerald McCarthy, *Five years in Ireland, 1895–1900,* Available online at: http://www.chaptersofdublin.com/books/General/victoria.htm (Accessed 28 December 2008).

12. P. Gatenby, *Dublin's Meath Hospital*, Dublin: Town House Press, 1996, p. 79.
13. Cited in *Adelaide Hospital Dublin One Hundred Years of Nursing, 1858-1958*, Dublin: Capital Press 1958, p. 14.
14. Anon., *Nursing Record & Hospital World*, 28 April 1900, p. 331.
15. Ibid.
16. Royal Dublin Fusiliers Association 2008, Available online at: http://www.greatwar.ie/postwar.html (Accessed 26 December 2008).
17. Ibid.
18. S. Horghan-Ryan, 'Irish military nurses in the Great War', In: Fealy G. M., *Care to Remember: Nursing and Midwifery in Ireland*, Cork: Mercier Press, 2005, 89-101
19. Royal Dublin Fusiliers Association 2008, op cit.
20. AHF/MS/MC/11270/63 Nurses' Biography 1877–1919.
21. Mitchell, *A Peculiar Place*, p. 151.
22. Ibid., p. 258.
23. National Library of Ireland, *The 1916 Rising: Personalities and Perspectives*, Available online at: http://www.nli.ie/1916/pdf/7.8.pdf (Accessed 28 December 2008).
24. Cumann na mBan (translated to English as the league of women) was a women's paramilitary group founded in 1913.
25. Bureau of Military History Document WS 204, National Archives, Available online at: http://www.nationalarchives.ie/topics/1916/WS204/2.html (Accessed 28 December 2008).
26. Ibid. Document WS 204, 822.
27. S. Ó Maitiú, *W&R Jacob: Celebrating 150 Years of Irish Biscuit Making*, Dublin: Woodfield Press, 2001.
28. Mitchel,l *A Peculiar Place*, p. 154.
29. McEwen, *Long Way to Tipperary*, Chapter 1.
30. M. E. Baly, *Nursing and Social Change* (Third Edition), London: Routledge, 1995.
31. House of Commons 1904, *Select Committee on the Registration of Nurses, together with the Proceedings of the Committee, Minutes of Evidence, Appendix and Index*, H.C. London: HMSO, 1904 (281) vi.701 and 1905 (263), p. iii.
32. MS/AHD/MC/11270/61, 1895–1906, 5 January 2004.
33. M. Vicinus, *Independent Women: Work and Community for Single Women, 1850-1920*, London: Virago, 1985, p. 115.
34. For an authoritative biography of Margaret Huxley, see Susan McGann, *The Battle of the Nurses: A Study of Eight Women Who Influenced the Development of Professional Nursing, 1880-1930*, London: Scutari Press, 1992.
35. T. P. C. Kirkpatrick, *Registration for Nurses: a Lecture Delivered in the Dublin Metropolitan Technical School for Nurses*, Dublin: University Press, 1917, p. 6.
36. Anon., *BJN*, 61, 21 September 1918, p. 182.
37. Ibid.
38. Margaret Huxley was elected Vice-chairman of the first General Nursing Council for Ireland. For an authoritative biography of Margaret Huxley, see Susan McGann, *Battle of the Nurses*. See also Fealy, Dublin Metropolitan Technical School.
39. Mitchell, *A Peculiar Place*, p. 257.
40. Anon., *BJN*, 64, 7 February 1920, p. 82.
41. Ibid.
42. Ibid.

CHAPTER FIVE

1. Department of Local Government and Public Health, *The Hospitals Commission: First General Report, 1933-4*, Dublin: The Stationery Office, 1936, p. 65.

2. M. E. Daly, 'An atmosphere of sturdy independence', in Malcolm E. and Jones G. (eds), *Medicine Disease and the State in Ireland 1650-1940*, Cork: Cork University Press, 1999, pp. 234-252.

3. O'Ferrall, *The Adelaide Hospital.*

4. House of Commons, *Nurses Registration (Ireland) Act,* HC: The Stationery Office, 1919, Clause 3, para. 1.

5. *Rules made under Nurses' Registration (Ireland) Act 1919*, Dublin: GNCI, 1920, Article II, parts 1 and 2.

6. Ibid.

7. General Nursing Council for Ireland (hereafter GNCI) *Regulations Made by the General Nursing Council,* Dublin: The Stationery Office, 1923.

8. MS Minutes of General Nursing Council for Ireland, Dublin: GNCI, 14 November, 1923.

9. Fealy, *Apprenticeship Training,* p. 111.

10. Cited in Mitchell, *A Peculiar Place,* p. 97.

11. Ibid.

12. G. M. Fealy, 'A place for the better technical education of nurses: the Dublin Metropolitan Technical School for Nurses, 1893-1969', *Nursing History Review,* 13, 2005, 27-43.

13. Mitchell, *A Peculiar Place,* p. 95.

14. Fealy, 'Dublin Metropolitan Technical School'.

15. Fealy, *Apprenticeship Training,* p. 97.

16. MS AHD/NC/11270/58, 22 January 1942.

17. The reason for this action is not indicated in the hospital archives.

18. MS AHD/NC/11270/58, 14 March 1944.

19. MS AHD/NC/11270/58, 16 November 1939.

20. AHF/MS/MC/11270/64/19, 1943-1974, 10 October 1939.

21. The tensions and conflicts among the senior nurses at this time merit further investigation.

22. AHD, *Twenty-fifth Annual Report of the Adelaide Hospital for the Year ending 31st December 1944,* Dublin: AHD, 1945, p. 19.

23. AHD *Twenty-eight Annual Report of the Adelaide Hospital for the Year ending 31st December 1947,* Dublin: AHD, 1948, p. 5.

24. MS, AHD/NC/11270/58, 5 October 1948.

25. Ibid.

26. Ibid.

27. Fealy, *Apprenticeship Training,* Chapter 7.

28. AHD, *Rules for Probationers and Nurses,* Dublin: The Adelaide Hospital, 1923, p. 6.

29. AHD, *Rules for Probationers and Nurses,* Dublin: Adelaide Hospital Dublin, 1942, p. 25.

30. MS AHD/NC/11270/58, 14 March 1944; Mitchell, *A Peculiar Place,* p. 159. Mrs Louise Bewley was a member of the Nursing Committee in the 1930s.

31. Ibid., 14 October 1944.

32. A. Bradshaw, *The Nurse Apprentice, 1860-1977,* Aldershot: Ashgate, 2001, pp. 88-89.

33. Ibid., p. 89.

34. AHD, *The Twelfth Annual Report of the Adelaide Hospital for the Year ending 31st December 1931,* Dublin: AHD, 1932, p. 19.

35. MS, AHD/NC/11270/58, 11 July 1939.

36. Fealy, *Apprenticeship Training,* Chapter 7.

37. Cited in Mitchell, *A Peculiar Place,* pp. 161 and 169.

38. Ibid., p. 97.

39. Fealy, *Apprenticeship Training,* 2006, p. 113.

40. Anon., *The Irish Nurses' Magazine*, 13 (33), 1944, p. 2.
41. Ibid.
42. Fealy, *Apprenticeship training*, pp. 113-6.
43. D. M, Dixon, 'A different approach to the nursing recruitment problem', *BJN*, 94, 1946, p. 115.
44. Anon., *The Irish Nurses' Magazine*, 12 (21), 1943, pp. 6-7.
45. Anon., *The Irish Nurses' Magazine*, 15 (8), 1948, p. 2.
46. MS AHD/NC/11270/58, 1946.
47. Testimony of Maureen Temple (nee Woods) (MT), 2008.
48. Ibid., p. 98.
49. Cited in Mitchell, *A Peculiar Place*, p. 100.
50. Testimony of MT, 2008.
51. MS AHD/NC/11270/58, 14 October 1944, 9 July 1940.
52. Ibid., 14 March 1944.
53 Testimony, MT, 2008.
54. Testimony of Lily Foxall (EF) (nee Nuzum), 2008.
55. Cited in Mitchell, *A Peculiar Place*, p. 98.
56. Testimony of Gertrude Jeffers (GJ). Gertrude Jeffers later became President of the Nurses' League and Matron of the Convalescent Home.
57. Testimony, MT.
58. Ibid.
59. Personal testimony of Phyllis Winslow (nee Noblett), 2008.
60. B. McBryde, *Quiet Heroines: Nurses of the Second World War*, London: Chatto & Windus, 1985, cited at QURANC, Available online at: http://www.qaranc.co.uk/damemar-gotturner.php (Accessed 12 February 2009).
61. League of Adelaide Hospital Nurses, *Bulletin*, Dublin: League of Adelaide Nurses, 1946.
62. QURANC, op cit.
63. Testimony of EF.
64. League of Adelaide Hospital Nurses, *Bulletin*, 1946 Dublin: League of Adelaide Nurses. I am grateful to Hilary Daly for giving me access to the Adelaide Hospital Nurses' League Annual reports, and for her ideas and suggestions about other aspects of the manuscript.
65. Adelaide Hospital (Incorporated) Nurses' League (hereafter AHNL), *Second and Third Annual Report 1947-1948*, Dublin: AHNL, p. 5.
66. Testimony of GJ, 2008.

CHAPTER SIX

1. J. Deeny, *The Irish Nurses Magazine*, 16 (11), 1949, pp. 2-5.
2. For a discussion on the background to the establishment of An Bord Altranais, see Fealy, *Apprenticeship Training*, pp. 118-121.
3. O'Ferrall, *Adelaide Hospital*, pp. 18-19.
4. Adelaide Hospital (Incorporated) Nurses' League (hereafter AHNL) *Eleventh Annual Report 1956*, Dublin: AHNL, p. 10.
5. Testimony, EF.
6. AHD, *The Twenty-ninth Annual Report of the Adelaide Hospital for the Year ending 31st December 1950*, Dublin: AHD, 1951, p. 5.
7. Mitchell, *A Peculiar Place*.
8. The hospitals of the Federation were the Adelaide, the Meath, the Royal City of Dublin, Sir Patrick Dun's, Mercer's, Dr Steevens, and the National Children's Hospital. The legislation to establish the federation was published as the Hospitals' Federation and

Amalgamation Act 1961.

9. AHD, *The Fifty-first Annual Report of the Adelaide Hospital for the Period 1st January 1970 to 31st March 1971*, Dublin: AHD, 1971, p. 8.

10. AHD, *The Fifty-second Annual Report of the Adelaide Hospital for the Period 1st April 1971 to 31st March 1972,* Dublin: AHD, 1972, p. 7.

11. Testimony, Y Seville (YS), November 2008.

12. Testimony of Joan FitzPatrick (JF), January 2009.

13. Ibid..

14. Testimony, YS.

15. Ibid.

16. Testimony, JF.

17. Testimony, YS.

18. Adelaide Hospital (Incorporated) Nurses' League (hereafter AHNL) *Eighteenth Annual Report 1963,* Dublin: AHNL, p. 7.

19. Testimony, YS.

20. Testimony Judith Chavasse (JC), 1998.

21. J. Chavasse, 'Nursing in the Emerald Isle', *International Nursing Review*, 15 (3), 1968, pp. 182-188.

22. J. Chavasse, 'Nursing: A career for life', *Association of Old Adelaide Students*, 1972, p. 12.

23. Testimony, GJ.

24. Testimony, JC.

25. Fealy, *Apprenticeship Training*, p. 138.

26. E. Hanrahan, *Report on the Training of Student Nurses,* Irish Matrons' Association, 1970, Chapter 5.

27. Fealy, *Apprenticeship Training*, p. 135.

28. Oral testimony was given by Sarah Condell (SC), Naomi Elliott (NE), Lily Foxall (nee Nuzum) (EF), Valerie Houlden (VH), Avril Brady (nee Shaw) AB, and Yvonne Seville (YS). Additional archival oral testimonies recorded in 1998 were consulted.

29. The term 'PTS' was widely used to refer to a first year student nurse, and is derived from Preliminary Training School.

30. Testimony of YS.

31. Ibid.

32. A snipe was a small bottle of Guinness.

33. Testimony, VH.

34. Testimony, YS.

35. Testimony, SC and VH.

36. Testimony, VH.

37. *An Bord Altranais News* 16 (2), p. 6; World of Irish Nursing 12 (5), Available online at: http://www.ino.ie/DesktopDefault.aspx?TabID=569 (Accessed 2 January 2009).

38. Testimony of Rhonda G. Kilpatrick (nee Rolston) (RR), 2008.

39. Ibid.

40. Testimony, VH.

41. Testimony, RR.

42. Ibid.

43. Testimony, JC.

44. Department of Health, *Working Party on General Nursing,* Dublin: The Stationery Office, 1980, p. 2. The Working Party was chaired by Brigid Tierney, the Senior Nurse Tutor at St James's Hospital and its Report was published 1980. See also J. Robins, 'An Bord Altranais after 1970', In Robins, J. (ed.), *Nursing and Midwifery in Ireland in the Twentieth Century*, Dublin: An Bord Altranais, 2000, p. 57.

45. AHD/MS/MC/11270/36.

46. AHD, *The Fifty-seventh Annual Report of the Adelaide Hospital for the Period Year Ending 31 December 1977*, Dublin: AHD, 1978 p. 5.

47. Ibid.

48. AHD, *The Fifty-ninth Annual Report of the Adelaide Hospital for the Period ending 31st December 1979*, Dublin: AHD, 1980, P.5.

49. Ibid., pp. 5 and 7.

CHAPTER SEVEN

1. AHD, *The Sixty-second Annual Report of the Adelaide Hospital for the Period ending 31st December 1981*, Dublin: AHD, 1982, p. 12.

2. Testimony of Avril Brady (nee Shaw) (AB), 2008.

3. The story of these fraught negotiations is well accounted for by historian Fergus O'Ferrall, and hence just a brief overview of the main developments is presented here. See F. O'Ferrall, 'The formation of the Adelaide and Meath Hospital, Dublin incorporating the National Children's Hospital', In Fitzpatrick, D. *The Feds: An Account of the Federated Dublin Voluntary Hospitals*, Dublin: A&A Farmer, 2006, pp. 43-52. See also F. O'Ferrall, 'A case study: The Adelaide and Meath Hospital Dublin, Incorporating the National Children's Hospital 1996-1999', in O'Ferrall, F., *Citizenship and Public Service: Voluntary and statutory Relationships in Irish Healthcare*, Dundalk: Dundalgan Press, pp. 161-224.

4. AHD, *The Sixty-second Annual Report of the Adelaide Hospital for the Period ending 31st December 1981*, Dublin: AHD, 1982, pp. 14-15; AHD 1980 *The Sixtieth Annual Report of the Adelaide Hospital for the Period ending 31st December 1979*, Dublin: AHD, p. 14.

5. Ibid., p. 16.

6. AHD, *The Sixty-first Annual Report of the Adelaide Hospital for the Period ending 31st December 1980*, Adelaide Hospital: Dublin, 1981, p. 13; AHD, *The Sixty-fifth Annual Report of the Adelaide Hospital for the Period ending 31st December 1984*, Dublin: AHD, 1985, p. 8.

7. AHD, Special meeting of the Nursing Committee, 12 July 1984, (insert in Annual Reports). Dublin: AHD.

8. Ibid.

9. An Bord Altranais, *Newsletter* 4 (1), 1987, pp. 1–2. The Central Applications Bureau was established on foot of a recommendation of the Working Party Report on General Nursing of 1980 and was provided for in the Nurses' Act of 1985.

10. AHD, *Annual Report of the Adelaide Hospital for the Period ending 31st December 1986*, Dublin: AHD, 1987, p. 7.

11. AHD, *Annual Report of the Adelaide Hospital for the Period ending 31st December 1987*, Dublin: AHD, 1988, p. 10.

12. AHD, *Annual Report of the Adelaide Hospital for the Period ending 31st December 1990*, Dublin: AHD, 1991, p. 12.

13. AHD, *Annual Report of the Adelaide Hospital for the Period ending 31st December 1992*, Dublin: AHD, 1993 p. 8.

14. AHD, *Annual Report of the Adelaide Hospital for the Period ending 31st December 1991*, Dublin: AHD, 1992, p. 7.

15. The Committee was chaired by Dr David Kennedy.

16. Ibid., p. 10.

17. AHD, *Annual Report of the Adelaide Hospital for the Period ending 31st December 1992*, Dublin: AHD, 1993, p. 13.

18. Idid., p. 7.

19. AHD, *Annual Report of the Adelaide Hospital for the Period ending 31st December 1993*, Dublin: AHD, 1995, p. 7.

20. AHD, *Annual Report of the Adelaide Hospital for the Period ending 31st December 1993,* Dublin: AHD, 1994.

21. The Working Part became known as the Kennedy-Kingston Working Party. Its co-chairmen were Dr David Kennedy and Mr David Kingston.

22. AHD, *Annual Report 1993,* 1994, p. 11.

23. Ibid.

24, Ibid., p. 10.

25. AHD, *Annual Report of the Adelaide Hospital for the Period ending 31st December 1988,* Dublin: AHD, p. 16.

26. AHD, *Annual Report of the Adelaide Hospital for the Period ending 31st December 1989,* Dublin: AHD, 1990, p. 15.

27. Ibid, p. 18.

28. AHD, *Annual Report of the Adelaide Hospital for the Period ending 31st December 1992,* Dublin: AHD, 1993, p. 8.

29. Ibid., p. 9.

30. Ibid.

31. Ibid.

32. Testimony, AB.

33. Testimony, NE.

34. Testimony, SC.

35. Aileen Henderick had been previously at the National Children's Hospital.

36. AHHNL, Annual reports.

37. The total number of students in training at any one time was 108, of which number 38 were in class almost all of the year.

38. Testimony, NE.

39. Fealy, *Apprenticeship Training,* pp. 142-143

40. Testimony, AB and SC.

41. An Bord Altranais, *Nurse Education and Training Consultative Document: Interim Report of the Review Committee,* Dublin: An Bord Altranais, 1991.

42. Initially located at St James's Hospital, the school moved to new premises at D'Olier Street in 2003.

43. An Bord Altranais, *The Future of Nurse Education and Training,* Dublin: An Bord Altranais, 1991, p. 13.

44. The Adelaide Hospital Society *Annual Report 1997,* Dublin: AHS, 1998, p. 4.

45. Government of Ireland (1998) *A Blueprint for the Future: Report of the Commission on Nursing,* Dublin: the Stationery Office. The Commission also examined midwifery in Ireland.

46. The Adelaide Hospital Society AHS *Annual Report,* Dublin: AHS 1999, p. 4.

CHAPTER EIGHT

1. Testimony of a former Adelaide nurse.

2. Adelaide Hospital Society, *Nurse Education through the Adelaide School of Nursing,* Dublin: AHS 2001, pp. 8 and 11.

3. For details of all publications of the Adelaide Hospital Society, see Adelaide Hospital Society, available at: http://www.adelaide.ie/index.php?id=16 (accessed 12 February 2009).

4. I am grateful to Dr Fergus O'Ferrall for his helpful remarks in the development of the closing passages of the manuscript concerning the Adelaide Hospital Society.

Index